MW01074896

THE NEWEST

FROM CALIFORNIA

THE NEWEST LOGO

FROM CALIFORNIA

2

PUBLISHED BY MADISON SQUARE PRESS

ISBN 0-942604-58-X
Library of Congress Catalog Card Number 97-072871

Distributors to the trade in the United States & Canada:
Watson-Guptill
1515 Broadway
New York, New York 10036

Distributed throughout the rest of the world by:
Hearst Books International
1350 Avenue of the Americas
New York, New York 10019

Published by:
Madison Square Press
10 East 23rd Street New York, New York 10010
Phone (212) 505-0950,   Fax: (212) 979-2207

Design by: Harish Patel Design, New York

ACKNOWLEDGMENTS

This series was started by Gerry Rosentswieg in 1992. Our collaboration lasted until his death in 1995. It was his inspiration and his inventiveness that allowed me the courage to attempt this project without him. For this and countless other kindnesses and dreams we shared, I thank him, publicly.

Printed in Hong Kong

Contents

designer   Jeanine Colini
illustrator   Patsy Tucker
design firm   Jeanine Colini Design
               Associates
client   Training With
               Tambourine
               Logo for animal
               behavioral specialists.

designer	Paul Weingartner
art directors	Steve Turner
	Joan Hausman
design firm	Hausman Design
client	Altera

Mark for a semi-conductor programming company.

designer	Paul Morales
design firm	Onyx Design Inc.
client	Birkenstock

Logo for back-to-school shoes and sandals.

(opposite)

designers	Larry Vigon
	Rowena Curtis
design firm	Vigon/Ellis
client	Can't Sing Can't Dance Productions

Logo for a television production company.

designer	Lissa Patrizi
design firm	Patrizi Designs
client	Jeff's Decorative Finishes

Logo for custom painting and art furniture.

Introduction

Before the world was filled with people who could read, pictures were used to replace words. Those who sold goods or services hung pictures depicting what they did over their doors. These, then, were the first brandmarks and the first logos. While these informational symbols (pictures) were a necessity for thousands of years, today we have more sophisticated ways of passing on the same information. The old signs are now much sought after as antiques or simply as pleasing wall decor.

As more of the goods and services we needed were offered by many more tradesmen it became important to be able to distinguish one maker from the next. Letters and words would do the trick but few were literate and, as in America, many were literate but in some other language. It was but a short step to using symbols to identify which tradesman had made which product or offered which service. They became easy to identify and sometimes carried a message for those who could read.

The earliest marks were very straightforward, but as more competition developed the mark expanded to include humor, puns, satire and even whimsy slipped into some. Fred Cooper's symbol for the New York Edison Company was dropped in the name

of progress, but Mr. Peanut is still with us and still looking through his monocle. Both were used to identify a product and both used a light touch.

Isaac Newton said "For every action there is reaction." It is also true that each period of art is a reaction to the period that preceded it. Graphic design is no exception. The styles favored in the late 1800s and the early 1900s were more like personal statements. The fine work done in France and England during the Edwardian era, along with the Viennese Secessionist movement, were all hands-on movements. With the Armistice came Art Deco, a style that captured the imagination with a cross between the mechanical shapes of the draftsman and the artist's irrepressible spirits.

As the great depression was ending, some remarkable marks began to appear. They were strong, clever, highly imaginative and subjective. They have stood the test of time very well and one would be hard pressed today to tell a mark created in 1936 from one right out of today's computer. Since that time the trademark has grown increasingly refined and distilled.

As the larger companies expanded into new and more diversified markets the graphics they chose became less related to the companies' beginnings and were in some cases abstract. The most used logos of the

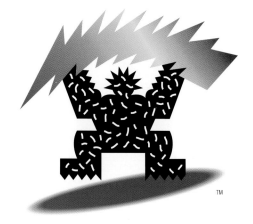

designer	Mamoru Shimokochi
art director	Anne Reeves
design firm	Shimokochi/Reeves
client	S/R Marketing Man Logo for identity and package design consultants.

time were difficult to identify— they were abstractions that reveal nothing about the identity of the company they represented.

Within the last decade things began to change. Humor and whimsy and the craft of graphic design began to slip back into the picture. The "NEW" logo is now, the marks are more quirky; what's new is beginning to look a lot like what's old. The charm and personality of the past has a decidedly "NOW" look and flavor. "NOW" is more eclectic, more colorful and more subjective.

As the nineties were starting to age, Rosentswieg was quoted as saying "The new logo is not necessarily a new phenomenon. There have always been those marks, usually created for small, creative companies that relied upon personality, wit and charm. Often the marks were created for designers and agencies for self promotion. But today, led by the music and entertainment industries, and followed closely by the clothing and computer industries, the NEW logo is appearing more often." These observations and ideas are now more mainstream; logos are again making a statement about whom or what they represent, and some of the world's largest companies now *believe.*

The Publisher

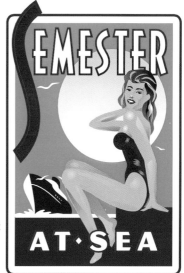

designer	Rod Dyer
design firm	Dyer/Mutchnick Group Inc.
client	Rooster Entertainment Group
	Logo for promoting the fun and romance of studying abroad.

1
designer   Glenn Sakamoto
art director   Rod Dyer
design firm   Dyer/Mutchnick Group Inc.
client   J.H. Rothschild, Inc.
               Logo for a set and prop designer.

2
designer   Glenn Martinez
design firm   Glenn Martinez and Associates
client   J.M. Hershey Inc.
               Logo for a general contractor
               specializing in church building and
               remodeling.

3
designer   Julia Chong Tam
design firm   Julia Tam Design
client   Italian Hotel Reservation Center
               Logo for tourist services.

4
designer   Konrad Bright
design firm   Bright Strategic Design
client   Folb Construction
               Logo for building contractors
               and management.

5
designer   Ron Miriello
illustrator   Michelle Aranda
design firm   Miriello Grafico, Inc.
client   National University
               Logo for the university.

6
designer   Cheryl Pelly
design firm   Pelly Design Associates
client   St. Maximillian Kolbe
               Logo for a church.

1

2

3   ITALIAN HOTEL
    RESERVATION CENTER

4

5

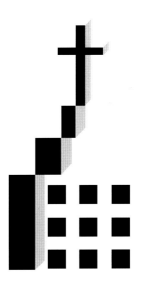

6

7
designer Cheryl Pelly
design firm Pelly Design Associates
client Citicopters News Service
Logo for news filming in
Los Angeles.

8
designer Eric Watanabe
art director Patti Judd
design firm Juddesign
client The Paragon Foundation
Logo for the parent company of
California Lutheran Homes and
Lutheran Social Services.

9
designer Archie Ong
design firm Inhaus Design
client Relocation Services
Logo for home relocation
services for employees of
large corporations.

10
designer Glenn Martinez
design firm Glenn Martinez and Associates
client Avalon Natural Cosmetics
Logo for a health and beauty
products company.

11
designer Konrad Bright
design firm Bright Strategic Design
client Terranova Construction
Logo for a construction company.

12
designers Philippe Becker
Primo Angeli
design firm Primo Angeli Inc.
client Rubin Glickman, Attorney
Logo highlights the landmark art
deco building that houses Rubin
Glickman's office.

13
designer Adrianna Dinihanian
design firm Pine Point Design
client Wrapworks
Logo for a take-out and
eat-in "wrap" (international
burrito) restaurant.

7

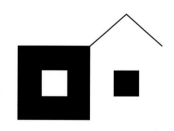

8 9

10

11

12

13

14
designer   Julia Chong Tam
design firm Julia Tam Design
client   AccuSight
              Logo for a laser eye care center.

15
designer   Richard Patterson
art director Mark Bergman
design firm SBG Partners
client   Brown & Towland
              Logo for a health care provider.

16
designers   Jeanne Namkung
              Anthony Luk
art directors Kenichi Nishiwaki
              Russell Baker
design firm Profile Design
client   FutureTel, Inc.
              Logo for a multi-media technology provider.

17
designer   Jeff Kahn
design firm Kahn Design
client   BioMax
              Logo for a colloidal nutritional
              supplement.

18
designer   Rod Dyer
design firm Dyer/Mutchnick Group Inc.
client   Sony Pictures High Definition Center
              Logo signifies one film process
              moving to the other.

14

AccuSight

BROWN & TOLAND
MEDICAL GROUP

15

FutureTel

16

BioMax™

17

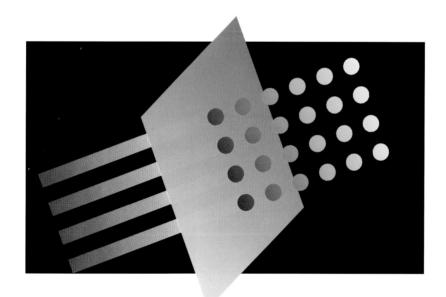

SONY PICTURES
HIGH DEFINITION CENTER

18

19

designer	Earl Gee
design firm	Gee + Chung Design
client	IBM Software Station
	Logo for an interactive kiosk which offers customers electronic delivery of software on-demand via satellite transmission.

20

designer	Paul Weingartner
art directors	Joan Hausman
	Steve Turner
design firm	Hausman Design
client	Metricom, Inc.
	Identity for a wireless communications company.

21

designers	Paul Weingartner
	Steve Turner
design firm	Hausman Design
client	Maxtor
	Marks for a disk drive company.

22

designer	Lynne Lukenbill
design firm	Digital Typography & Design
client	Data Marketing Inc.
	Logo for a direct mail marketing firm.

23

designer	Paul Weingartner
art directors	Steve Turner
	Joan Hausman
design firm	Hausman Design
client	Altera
	Mark for a semi-conductor programming company.

SOFTWARE STATION™

19

20

21

D A T A   M A R K E T I N G   I N C.

22

23

24
designer   John Ball
design firm   Mires Design
client   STAC
               Logo for a software company.

25
designer   Alexander Atkins
design firm   Alexander Atkins Design, Inc.
client   Alexander Atkins Design, Inc.
               Logo for a graphic design studio.

26
designer   Earl Gee
art director   Fani Chung
design firm   Gee + Chung Design
client   Vitria Technology, Inc.
               Logo for a high technology
               consulting firm providing
               information systems for large
               multinational corporations and
               government agencies.

27
designers   Edoardo Chavarin
               Larimie Garcia
design firm   gig
client   Innovation Snowboards
               Logo for a snowboard
               manufacturer.

28
designer   Larimie Garcia
design firm   gig
client   Swiss Jesus
               Logo for a musical group.

24

25

26

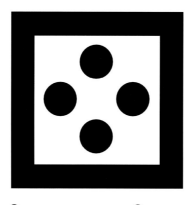

innovation
S N O W B O A R D S

27

28

29
designer   Glenn Martinez
design firm   Glenn Martinez and Associates
client   Stellar Ceramics
              Logo for a ceramic tile
              manufacturer.

30
designers   Larry Vigon
              Brian Jackson
design firm   Vigon/Ellis
client   Bridgwater Consulting Group
              Logo for a technology
              consulting group.

31
designers   Larry Vigon
              Marc Yeh
design firm   Vigon/Ellis
client   Century Housing Corporation
              Logo for a low-income housing
              financier and developer.

32
designer   Daren L. Passolt
design firm   Visualizer Design Studios
client   Spectris
              Badge logo created for Spectris
              mainframe computers.

33
designers   Larry Vigon
              Marc Yeh
design firm   Vigon/Ellis
client   Day Info
              Logo for an Australian
              software company.

34
designer   Steve Twigger
art director Rod Dyer
design firm   Dyer/Mutchnick Group Inc.
client   Logo for a cable TV Network that
              runs infomercials.

29

30

31

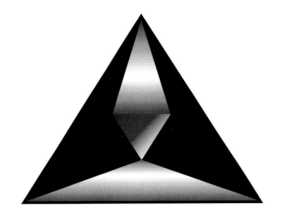

S P E C T R I S

32

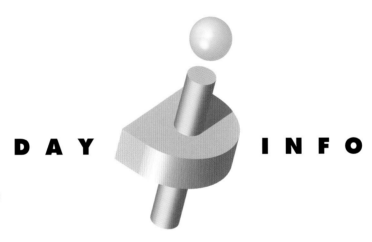

D A Y   **I N F O**

33

PIN ™

PRODUCT
INFORMATION
NETWORK

34

35
designer	Cheryl Pelly
design firm	Designworks/USA
client	BMW NA

Logo for a worldwide BMW conference for vendors held in Tucson, Arizona.

36
designer	Darryl Glass
art director	Lauren Bruhn
design firm	Laura Coe Design Associates
client	John Schulz Photography

Logo for a corporate photographer.

37
designer	Glenn Martinez
design firm	Glenn Martinez and Associates
client	Sonoma County AIDS Memorial

38
designers	Larry Vigon
	Rowena Curtis
design firm	Vigon/Ellis
client	Can't Sing Can't Dance Productions

Logo for a television production company.

39
designer	Martha Newton Furman
design firm	Martha Newton Furman Design & Illustration
client	Martha Newton Furman Design & Illustration

Logo for a design and illustration firm.

40
designer	Daren L. Passolt
design firm	Visualizer Design Studios
client	Visualizer Design Studios

Self-promotional logo/badge, created for embroidered baseball hats and T-Shirts.

35

36

37

IN OUR HEARTS FOREVER

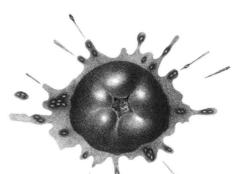

CAN'T SING CAN'T DANCE

PRODUCTIONS

38

39

40   v i s u a l i z e r

41
designer	Margo Chase
design firm	Margo Chase Design
client	Kemper Snowboards
	Product identity for Kemper Snowboards.

42
designer	Julia Chong Tam
design firm	Julia Tam Design
client	Milestones
	Logo for a greeting card company.

43
designer	Christopher Cantley
art director	Rod Dyer
design firm	Dyer/Mutchnick Group Inc.
client	New Star Pictures
	Logo for a motion picture production company.

44
designer	Edoardo Chavarin
design firm	gig
	Logo for a non-profit organization for human rights at the border of Mexico and the United States.

45
designer	Steve Turner
art director	Steve Turner
illustrator	Jae Shim
design firm	Hausman Design
client	California Water Service Company
	Identity for a water utility company.

41

42

43

44

45

46
designer Cheryl Pelly
design firm Pelly Design Associates
client David A. Steputis, D.D.S.
Logo for a dentist.

47
art director Rod Dyer
design firm Dyer/Mutchnick Group Inc.
client Leo Burnett/Sony
Retail logo for Sony Surround Sound.

48
designer Laura Mische
art directors Linda Warren
Monty House
design firm Warren Group
client Tektronix
Logo for a global
high-technology company.

49
designer Mamoru Shimokochi
art director Anne Reeves
design firm Shimokochi/Reeves
client UCLA
Logo for the 50th anniversary of the school
of theater, film and television at UCLA.

50
designer Daren L. Passolt
design firm Visualizer Design Studios
client Manufacturing Education
Logo created for manufacturing education
service provider.

51
designers Larry Vigon
Brian Jackson
illustrator Steve Berman
design firm Vigon/Ellis
client Rangers
Logo for a die casting company.

David A. Steputis, D.D.S.

46

SONY MAXIMUM TELEVISION™

47

48

UCLA

SCHOOL OF THEATER
FILM AND TELEVISION

1947 - 1997

50th

49

EDUCATION

50

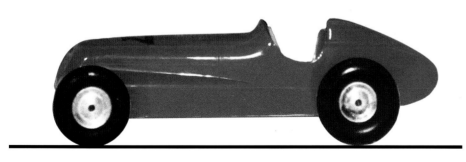

R A N G E R S

51

52
designers   Larry Vigon
             Brian Jackson
design firm Vigon/Ellis
client H_2O
             Logo for a water supply company
             for film studios.

53
designers   Larry Vigon
             Brian Jackson
design firm Vigon/Ellis
client   Sin-Drome Ltd.
             Logo for a record
             production company.

54
designer   Linda Kahn
art director Chip Clark
design firm Kahn Artist Design
client   Chip Clark Engineering

55
designer   Mark Kawakami
design firm M-Studios
client   Honda
             Logo for Honda's
             motorcycle division.

56
designer   John Ball
illustrator Miguel Perez
design firm Mires Design
client   McGraw Hill Home Interactive
             Logo for a CD Rom publisher.

57
designer   Mamoru Shimokochi
art director Anne Reeves
design firm Shimokochi/Reeves
client   X-Century
             Logo for a production studio
             in Japan.

58
designer   Jeff Kahn
art director Susan Tate
design firm Kahn Design
client   Revlon
             Logo for a botanical oil
             cosmetic product.

59
designer   Michael Stinson
design firm Stinson Design
client   Sinomex
             Logo for a Chinese owned business
             located in Mexico.

52

SIN·DROME
RECORDS LT

53

54

55

56

57

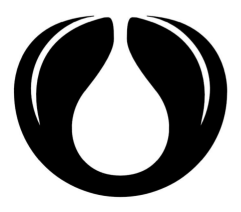

58

59

60
designer	Alexander Atkins
design firm	Alexander Atkins Design, Inc.
client	Stanford Business School Alumni Association
	Logo for organization providing activities, services and benefits to alumni.

61
designer	Cheryl Pelly
design firm	Pelly Design Associates
client	Las Calidas
	Logo for a Mexican resort.

62
designer	John White
illustrator	Jerry Lofquist
design firm	White Design, Inc.
client	National Physicians Network
	Logo for a multi-specialty medical group.

63
designer	Glenn Martinez
design firm	Glenn Martinez and Associates
client	virtual HeadQuarters
	Logo for a software company.

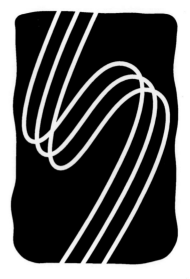

STANFORD BUSINESS SCHOOL ALUMNI ASSOCIATION

60

61

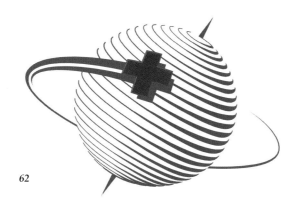

62

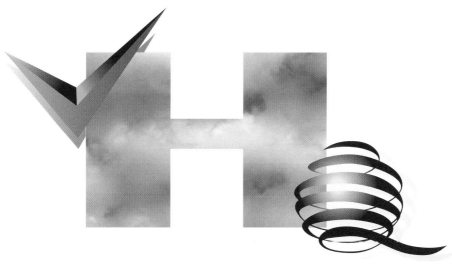

63

64

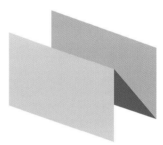

NOTEWORTHY

65

Disney**Interactive**

66

Together we're the best.
Los Angeles.

68

69

70

71

72

73

designer	Ryoichi Yotsumoto
art director	Laura Coe Wright
design firm	Laura Coe Design Associates
client	Sport Sling

Logo for soccer gear bags.

74

designer	Jann Bielenberg
illustrator	Eric David
design firm	Bielenberg Design Group
client	The Cassie Awards

Logo for the telecast awards show for the casino/resort entertainment industry.

75

designer	Douglas Bogner
art directors	Syndine Imholte
	Joanne McGowen
design firm	Bullzye Design & Marketing
client	Aon Consulting Inc.

Logo for an insurance and compensation brokerage company, consultants to businesses.

76

designer	Douglas Bogner
design firm	Bullzye Design & Marketing
client	The Tutoring Center

Logo for a company's stationery, collateral and signage.

77

designer	Laurel Bigley Mathe
art director	Paul Page
illustrator	Laura Zugzda
design firm	Page Design, Inc.
client	Chocoholics Devine Desserts

Logo for makers of chocolate sauce, chocolate pasta, etc.

73

74

75

76

77

78

designers	MaryAnn Mastrandrea
	Primo Angeli
art directors	Carlo Pagoda
	Richard Scheve
design firm	Primo Angeli Inc.
client	Beer Gear

Logo for a line of clothing for BrewMakers, a do-it-yourself beer brewery.

79

designer	Konrad Bright
design firm	Bright Strategic Design
client	Peter Miller Photography and Film

Logo for a still and motion picture photographer.

80

designer	Russell Leong
design firm	Russell Leong Design
client	Chris Brightman

Logo for a lighting designer and manufacturer.

81

designer	Russell Leong
illustrator	Mark Fox
design firm	Russell Leong Design
client	Worksmart Technologies

Logo for a new class of PC-based software that automates routine tasks associated with the retrieval and delivery of information.

82

designer	Jon Lagda
art director	Ron Scheibel
design firm	Hunt, Rook & Scheibel
client	SSE Foods Inc.

Proposed logo for a frozen food manufacturer.

83

designer	Peter Nam
design firm	Peter Nam Design
client	Taste Vacations

Logo for a line of exotic condiments.

78

79

80

81

82

83

84

designer	Diane Kuntz
design firm	Diane Kuntz Design
client	An Evening in Rio
	Logo for a fund-raising event for a local hospital.

85

designer	Jim Wylie
design firm	B-Square
client	Southern Gourmet Cookie Company
	Logo for a small gourmet cookie company.

86

designer	Paul Morales
design firm	Onyx Design Inc.
client	Birkenstock
	Logo for back-to-school shoes and sandals.

87

designer	Miles Beller
design firm	Beller Design
client	Homefront Broadcasting
	Logo for an internet start-up company looking to bring radio transmissions to the net.

88

designer	Paul Morales
design firm	Onyx Design Inc.
client	La Raza Centro Legao, Inc.
	Logo for a social service law agency's fund-raising dinner.

89

designer	Laurel Bigley Mathe
art director	Paul Page
design firm	Page Design, Inc.
client	Tasty Pockets
	Logo for a manufacturer of food products.

84

85

86

87

88

89

90

designer	Howard Ian Schiller
design firm	Designwise
client	Mobile Video
	Logo for a video rental store.

91

designer	Konrad Bright
design firm	Bright Strategic Design
client	Lopez Electric
	Logo for an electrical contractor.

92

designer	Barbara Brown
design firm	Barbara Brown Marketing and Design
client	Ventura County Medical Resource Foundation
	Logo for a foundation that provides medical and financial support for the local medical community.

93

designer	Debbie Smith
art director	David Leong
design firm	Addis Group
client	Holland Brothers
	Logo for a manufacturer of quality-crafted leather goods.

94

designer	Ray Wood
art director	Keith Bright
design firm	Bright Strategic Design
client	Wok Fast
	Logo for a fast food Chinese restaurant.

95

designer	Diane Kuntz
design firm	Diane Kuntz Design
client	CREST
	Logo for a citywide childcare/afterschool program.

90

91

LOPEZ ELECTRIC

92

HOLLAND
BROTHERS™

HANDMADE IN AMERICA

93

94

95

96
designer   Diane Kuntz
dillustrator April Bryant
design firm Diane Kuntz Design
client   California Hospital Medical Center
Logo for the medical center.

97
designer   Diane Kuntz
dillustrator Linda Eberle
design firm Diane Kuntz Design
client   Grand Hope Neonatology
Group Inc.
Logo for the NICU unit at California
Hospital Medical Center.

98
designer   Kimberly Lentz Powell
art director Doug Akagi
design firm Akagi Remington
client   Janice Tomita P.T. and Associates
Logo for a physical therapist.

99
designer   Konrad Bright
design firm Bright Strategic Design
client   Moffit Productions
Logo for a line of videos on
swimming.

100
designer   Jane McCambell
art director Doug Akagi
design firm Akagi Remington
client   Paul Margolies
Logo for a photographer.

101
designer   Becca Smidt
design firm Becca Smidt
client   Maitri Aids Hospice
Logo for a home for people
with Aids.

96

97

98

99

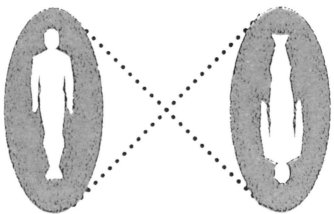

100

101

102
designer   Jeni Olsen
art director Nancy Daniels
design firm   The GNU Group
client   Muju Resort
                Logo for one of various Muju
                resorts in Korea.

103
designer   Jeni Olsen
art director Nancy Daniels
design firm   The GNU Group
client   Muju Resort
                Logo for one of various Muju
                resorts in Korea.

104
designer   Jeni Olsen
art director Nancy Daniels
design firm   The GNU Group
client   Muju Resort
                Logo for one of various Muju
                resorts in Korea.

105
designer   Paul Weingartner
design firm   pw Design
client   Second Harvest Food Bank
                Logo for a non-profit food bank for
                families in need.

106
designer   Brad Maur
design firm   Page Design, Inc.
client   Corporate Learning Center
                Logo for an educational division of
                the Money Store.

107
designer   Rod Dyer
illustrator   Andy Engel
design firm   Dyer/Mutchnick Group Inc.
client   Maverick
                Logo for an entertainment
                company.

102

103

104

105

106

107

108
designer	Brad Maur
design firm	Page Design, Inc.
client	Reebock

Logo for a manufacturer of outdoor footwear and clothing.

109
designer	Qris Yamashita
art director	Rod Dyer
design firm	Dyer/Mutchnick Group Inc.
client	Pivot Tour

Logo for a tour organizer/travel agency.

110
designers	Larry Vigon
	Brian Jackson
illustrator	Julie Dennis
design firm	Vigon/Ellis
client	Friedland Jacobs Communications

Logo for an entertainment advertising agency.

111
designer	Mike Brower
design firm	Mires Design
client	Bod-e

Logo for a personal health and fitness trainer.

112
designer	Jon Lagda
design firm	K3 Kato Kreative Koncepts
client	CSULB Performing Arts Center

Logo for a performing arts center.

113
designer	Jeff Kahn
design firm	Kahn Design
client	Puddle Dancer Press

Logo for a publisher of inspirational, spiritual and recovery-oriented books.

114
designers	Larry Vigon
	Brian Jackson
design firm	Vigon/Ellis
client	The Mad Platter

Logo for a caterer.

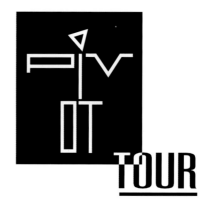

108

109

110

PERFORMING
ARTS CENTER
C S U L B

PuddleDancer PRESS ™

111   112   113

114

115
designer   Peter Sargent
art director   Greg Berman
design firm   Sargent & Berman
client   BoyerSports
Logo for an importer of fine
cycling accessories.

116
designer   Glenn Sakamoto
art director   Rod Dyer
design firm   Dyer/Mutchnick Group Inc.
client   Talent Entertainment Management
Logo for the company creates a
"human" manager.

117
designer   Linda Kahn
art director   Micki Wilson
design firm   Frank Templeton Inc.
client   Micki Wilson/Franklin
Templeton Inc.
Logo for innovative software to
speed up common tasks.

118
designer   Hun Wynn
art director   Rod Dyer
design firm   Dyer/Mutchnick Group Inc.
client   By Storm Entertainment
Logo for a music label.

119
designer   William Kent
art director   Tricia Rauen
design firm   Buz Design Group
client   Adelson Entertainment
Logo for entertainment
productions.

B O Y E R S P O R T S

115

TALENT ENTERTAINMENT MANAGEMENT

116

117

118 **BY STORM**™ **ENTERTAINMENT**

119 **adelson** entertainment

120
designers   Larry Vigon
             Brian Jackson
design firm Vigon/Ellis
client   Zoë
             Logo for a Pilates exercise studio.

121
designer   Steven Morris
design firm Steven Morris Design
client   Harvest Earth Fair
             Logo for a festival for
             environmentalism.

122
designer   Larry Vigon
illustrator Marc Yeh
design firm Vigon/Ellis
client   Max
             Logo for an online
             production resource.

123
designer   Rod Dyer
design firm Dyer/Mutchnick Group Inc.
client   Rooster Entertainment Group
             Logo for promoting the fun and
             romance of studying abroad.

120

121

122

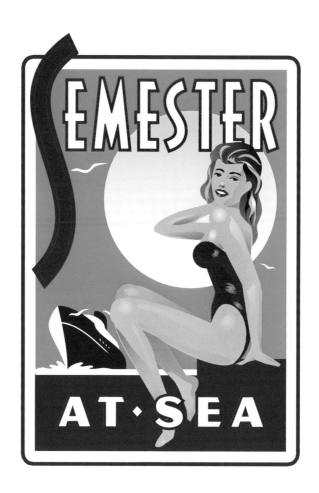

123

124
designers	Marcelo De Freitas
	Primo Angeli
art director	Carlo Pagoda
design firm	Primo Angeli Inc.
client	San Francisco Film Society
	Logo for the San Francisco International Film Festival.

125
designer	Michael Stinson
design firm	Kelston International, Inc.
client	Centor
	Logo for manufacturer and producer of CD Rom database software for optimum retrieval.

126
designer	Michael Stinson
design firm	Kelston International, Inc.
client	Centor
	Logo for a manufacturer and producer of CD Rom database software for optimum retrieval.

127
designer	Mamoru Shimokochi
art director	Anne Reeves
design firm	Shimokochi/Reeves
client	S/R Marketing Man
	Logo for identity and package design consultants.

124

125

126

127

™

128
designer   John Smeaton
art director Scott A. Mednick
design firm   Think New Ideas
client   ECO Halloween Bash
              Logo for an environmental
              group in Hollywood..

129
designer   José A. Serrano
illustrator   Tracy Sabin
design firm   Mires Design
client   Nike
              Logo for Nike, Deion Sanders
              cross-training shoes.

130
designer   Michael Stinson
design firm   Stinson Design
client   Autokickers!
              Logo for an adolescent
              paintball team.

131
designer   Julie Ann Stricklin
design firm   The Stricklin Companies
client   Nickel Slick
              Logo for a rock and roll band.

132
designer   Lissa Patrizi
design firm   Patrizi Designs
client   The Wright Touch
              Logo for decorative painting and
              architectural painting and finishes.

133
designer   Deborah Hom
art director José A. Serrano
illustrator   Tracy Sabin
design firm   Mires Design
client   Industry Pictures
              Logo for a motion picture
              company.

128

129

130

131

132

133

134
designer   Daren L. Passolt
design firm Visualizer Design Studios
client   Raymac
             Logo created for custom made
             bicycle frames.

135
designer   Larimie Garcia
design firm gig
client   Sin Sity
             Logo for an adult video and
             accessory store.

136
designer   Jefrey Gunion
design firm Jefrey Gunion Illustration & Design
client   The Electric Library
             Logo for an online "library" service
             with powerful search engine.

137
designer   Arne Ratermanis
design firm Arne Ratermanis
client   One Singles Club
             Logo for a singles club.

138
designer   Arne Ratermanis
design firm Lorenz Advertising & Design, Inc.
client   CST Images
             Logo for a software developer
             specializing in programs that
             reduce software development time.

139
designer   Laurel Bigley Mathe
art director   Paul Page
illustrator   Laura Zugzda
design firm   Page Design, Inc.
client   Harlow's
                Logo for an Italian restaurant with a
                1930s theme.

140
designer   Alexander Atkins
design firm Alexander Atkins Design, Inc.
client   Lindstrom Represents
             Logo for company
             representing artists.

134

135

136

SINGLES CLUB

137

CST Images

138

MODERN ITALIAN

139

140

141
designers   Larry Vigon
               Brian Jackson
illustrator   Denise Milford
design firm Vigon/Ellis
client   Clive Wilkinson Architecture
               Logo for an architect.

142
designer   Martha Newton Furman
design firm Martha Newton Furman
               Design & Illustration
client   Martha Newton Furman Design &
               Illustration
               Icon created to promote the
               designer/illustrator.

143
designer   Mark Allen
art director Trish Burke
design firm Mark Allen Design
client   Dumb & Dumber
               Logo for Dumb & Dumber
               TV show merchandise.

144
designer   Mike Salisbury
illustrator   Dave Willardson
design firm Mike Salisbury
               Communications, Inc.
client   Powerhouse
               Logo for a full service,
               state-of-the-art digital and
               conventional service bureau.

145
designer   Brad Maur
design firm Page Design, Inc.
client   Reebok
               Logo for an outdoor footwear and
               clothing manufacturer.

146
designers   Mark Jones
               Terrence Tong
art directors Carlo Pagoda
               Nina Dietzel
design firm Primo Angeli Inc.
client   Noah's Bagels
               Logo for bagel outlets.

141

142

143

144

145

146

147
designer Jeff Ivarson
design firm Ivarson Design Group
client Roughneck
Logo for a manufacturer of
fishing rods.

148
designer Jefrey Gunion
design firm Jefrey Gunion Illustration & Design
client Advanced Communications Group
Logo for a high level
communication techniques training
and consultation group.

149
designer John Smeaton
art director Scott A. Mednick
design firm Think New Ideas
client Guys Tuys
Logo for a manufacturer of
designer ties.

150
designer Daren L. Passolt
design firm Visualizer Design Studios
client American Cyclist
Logo for custom made bicycle
frames and components.

151
designer Rose Hartono
art director Tricia Rauen
design firm Buz Design Group
client Node Warrior Networks
Logo for an internet server.

147

148

149

150

151

152
designer Qris Yamashita
art director Rod Dyer
design firm Dyer/Mutchnick Group Inc.
client J B Music Publishing LLC
Logo for a hip music
publishing company.

153
designer Alexander Atkins
design firm Alexander Atkins Design, Inc.
client Abbott Usability
Logo for company conducting
product evaluations.

154
designer Mark Kawakami
design firm M-Studios
client Quiksilver Eyewear
Logo for a manufacturer of
sunglasses.

155
designer Jeff Yeh
art director Ron Scheibel
design firm Hunt, Rook & Scheibel
client Hunt, Rook & Scheibel
Logo for an advertising agency.

156
designers Doug Akagi
Lorsen Koo
art director Doug Akagi
design firm Akagi Remington
client Freestyle
Logo for a fast food franchise.

152

ABBOTT
USABILITY

153

EYEWEAR

154

155

156

157
designer Paul Weingartner
design firm pw Design
client Allen Hadley, CMT
Logo for a personal masseur.

158
designer Paul Weingartner
design firm pw Design
client Castro Village Pharmacy
Logo for a pharmacy.

159
designer Bill Kent
art director Tricia Rauen
design firm Buz Design Group
client Adelson Entertainment
Logo for entertainment
productions.

160
designer Jeanine Colini
illustrator Patsy Tucker
design firm Jeanine Colini Design Associates
client Training With Tambourine
Logo for animal behavioral
specialists.

161
designer Darlene McElroy
design firm Darlene McElroy Design
client Karen McKee
Logo for an art therapist.

157

158

159

160

KAREN • McKEE

Art Therapist

161

162
designer	Ray Wood
art director	Keith Bright
design firm	Bright Strategic Design
client	South Park Sports Stadium Group

Logo for a sports group formed to bring a new state-of-the-art football stadium to Los Angeles.

163
designer	Konrad Bright
design firm	Bright Strategic Design
client	Danny Sullivan Inc.

Logo for a race car company.

164
designer	Julia Chong Tam
design firm	Julia Tam Design
client	SBJT

Logo for a youth tennis league.

165
designer	Dana Lamb
design firm	Sleepy Hollow Design
client	Chino Unified School District

Pro-bono logo for a children's athletic competition to raise money for art programs.

166
designer	Ryoichi Yotsumoto
art director	Laura Coe Wright
design firm	Laura Coe Design Associates
client	The Active Foot

Logo for direct mail running shoe sales.

167
designers	José Serrano
	Mark Mattingly
illustrator	Mark Mattingly
design firm	Mires Design
client	Hage Elementary

Logo for a promotional T-shirt given away to children who belonged to the school's chess club.

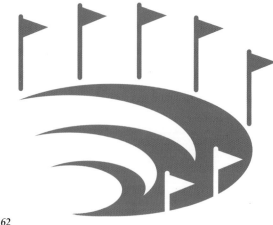

162

163

164

165

166

167

168
designer   Daren L. Passolt
design firm   Visualizer Design Studios
client   Stanford University/Amdahl
               Corporation
               Created for an educational InRoads
               Challenge Program, sponsored
               by Amdahl Corporation and
               Stanford University.

169
designer   Vicki Wyatt
art director   Patti Judd
design firm   Juddesign
client   Sun 'n' Sand
               Logo for a volleyball sportswear
               manufacturer.

170
designer   José A. Serrano
art director   Miguel Perez
illustrator   Carl Vanderschuit
design firm   Mires Design
client   Voit Sports
               Logo for a project to introduce a
               brand new line of ball with a
               unique grip.

171
designer   Bradley W. Grose
design firm   Bradley Grose Design
client   Pasadena Rose Bowl
               Logo for the World Cup
               opening ceremony.

172
designer   Scott Mires
illustrator   Tracy Sabin
design firm   Mires Design
client   LA Gear
               Logo for a footwear product line.

173
designers   Miguel Perez
               Scott Mires
design firm   Mires Design
client   Nike
               Logo for Michael Jordon's
               retirement celebration.

168

169

170

171

172

173

174
designer   Cheryl Gillis
art directors Greg Berman
            Peter Sargent
design firm Princess Cruises
client   L.A. Care Health Plan
            Logo for the cruise ship
            Dawn Princess.

175
designer   Carol Gravelle
art directors Carol Gravelle
            David Wood
design firm Carol Gravelle Graphic Design
client   Xircom
            Logo for sales incentive program
            for networking products.

176
designer   Julia Chong Tam
design firm Julia Tam Design
client   Hellenic American Cruises
            Logo for a cruise ship of
            two countries.

177
designer   Peter Sargent
art director Greg Berman
design firm Sargent & Berman
client   Breaking Away
            Logo for a bicycle touring company.

178
designer   Riki Komachi
design firm Riki Komachi
client   Bikes For Cops
            Logo for joint effort of Venice police
            and sheriff to buy more bikes for
            patrol.

174

175

176

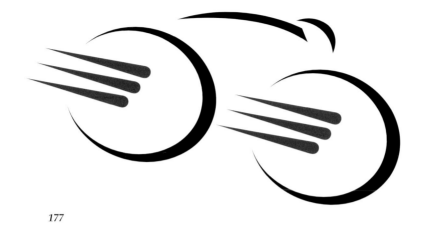

177

178

179
designer	Bradley W. Grose
art director	Charlie Shaw
design firm	Bradley Grose Design
client	Pat Boone

Logo for a poster commemorating the 40th anniversary of Pat Boone's first million-selling song, "Ain't That a Shame."

180
designer	Bradley W. Grose
design firm	Bradley Grose Design
client	Hughes Aircraft Corporation

Logo for Naval Air Weapons Command counter measures receiving set.

181
designer	Bradley W. Grose
art director	Tim Ramos
design firm	Bradley Grose Design
client	Disney Home Video

New packaging logo for Vintage Disney Cartoon Classics.

182
designer	Bradley W. Grose
design firm	Bradley Grose Design

Logo for WWII ace Colonel Herschel H. Green.

183
designer	Bradley W. Grose
design firm	Bradley Grose Design
client	Edwards Air Force Base, Southern California

Logo for the 50th anniversary of America's first jet flight.

184
designer	Bradley W. Grose
design firm	Bradley Grose Design
client	United States Navy/Jet Pioneers of the U.S.A.

Logo for the U.S. Navy's 50th anniversary of the first jet propelled carrier take-off and landing.

179

180

181

182

183

184

185
art director   Tricia Rauen
design firm   Buz Design Group
client   Rockwell Federal Credit Union
Logo for a kids' banking program.

186
art director   Tricia Rauen
design firm   Buz Design Group
client   Rockwell Federal Credit Union
Logo for a kids' banking program.

187
designer   Laurel Bigley Mathe
art director   Paul Page
design firm   Page Design, Inc.

188
designer   Barbara D. Cummings
art director   David Parker
design firm   DAA
client   Caribbean Traders
Logo for retailers of adventurous
lifestyle gear.

189
designer   Michael Ketz
illustrator   Jennifer Hewitson
design firm   Hetz Advertising & Design
client   Ark Enterprises
Logo for a marketing and public
relations firm.

190
designer   Dana Lamb
art director   Steve Forbes
design firm   Sleepy Hollow Design
client   Ingram-Micro, Inc.
Logo for an Ingram-Micro
promotional campaign for Apple
Macintosh product line.

185

186

187

188

189

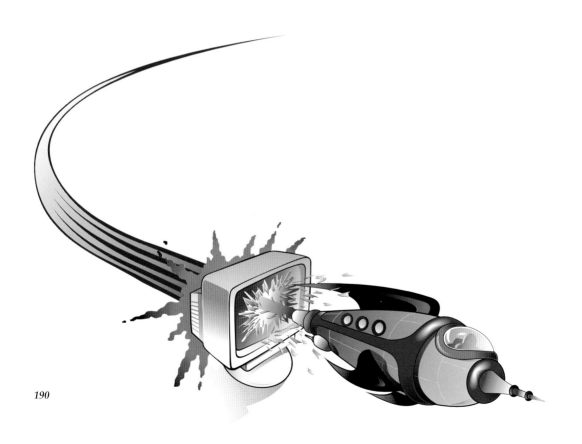

190

191
designer | Jay Galster
art director | Jerry Takigawa
design firm | Jerry Takigawa Design
client | ColorAd Printers
Logo for a printer.

192
designer | Gregory Thomas
design firm | Gregory Thomas Associates
client | Monarch Pictures
Logo for a division of Tristar Pictures.

193
designer | Martha Newton Furman
design firm | Martha Newton Furman Design & Illustration
client | Martha Newton Furman Design & Illustration
Logo for a holiday greeting card.

194
designer | Margo Chase
design firm | Margo Chase Design
client | Kemper Snowboards
Product identity for Kemper Snowboards.

195
designer | Ryoichi Yotsumoto
art director | Laura Coe Wright
design firm | Laura Coe Design Associates
client | Peregrine Solutions
Logo for a law firm that specializes in legal defense cost management.

196
designer | Ray Wood
design firm | Bright Strategic Design
client | NATPE
Logo for a professional association of television producers and executives.

191

192

193

194

195

196

197-201
designer   Corinne Char
art director   Nancy Daniels
design firm   The GNU Group
client   Deer Valley Center
    Logos for a neighborhood shopping
    center in Phoenix, Arizona.

DEER VALLEY CENTER

197

198

199

200

201

202

designer	Jon Lagda
art director	Ron Scheibel
design firm	Hunt, Rook & Scheibel
client	Roosters

Proposed logo for a distributor of frozen breakfast entrees.

203

designer	Jeff Yeh
art director	Ron Scheibel
design firm	Hunt, Rook & Scheibel
client	Cock-A-Doodle Doos

Logo for a maker of breakfast food items.

204

designer	Sarah Tannas
art director	Ron Scheibel
design firm	Hunt, Rook & Scheibel
client	Coyote Grill

Proposed logo for a line of Southwestern entrees.

205

designer	Jeanine Colini
illustrator	Jeanine Colini
design firm	Jeanine Colini Design Associates
client	Greater Los Angeles Zoo Association

Logo for an annual fund raising benefit for the Los Angeles Zoo.

206

designer	Jeanine Colini
illustrator	Jeanine Colini
design firm	Jeanine Colini Design Associates
client	Colini + Company

Logo for the sale and promotion of the "A to Zoo" poster which consists of 26 illustrated animal characters.

202

203

204

BEASTLY BALL

205

A to ZOO

206

207
designer   Carol Gravelle
art directors Carol Gravelle
             Barbara Mizuno
design firm Mizuno & Associates
client   Weider
             Logo for bodybuilding and
             fitness products.

208
designer   Barbara Brown
design firm Barbara Brown Marketing and
             Design
client   Spot Satellite
             Logo intended to communicate
             company's desire to "sit up,
             roll over and fetch."

209
designer   Gerald Reis
illustrator   Susan Greinetz
design firm Gerald Reis Design Studio
client   Lindsay Wildlife Museum
             Logo for a museum committed to
             the welfare of the natural world.

210
designer   Kimberly Lentz Powell
art director Doug Akagi
design firm Akagi Remington
client   Sun Fun
             Logo for children's and maternity
             clothing stores

211
designer   Glenn Martinez
design firm Glenn Martinez and Associates
client   Avalon Natural Cosmetics
             Logo for a health and beauty
             products company.

212
designer   Glenn Martinez
design firm Glenn Martinez and Associates
client   American Red Cross
             Logo for a fashion show and
             auction to benefit Red Cross.

207

208

209

210

211

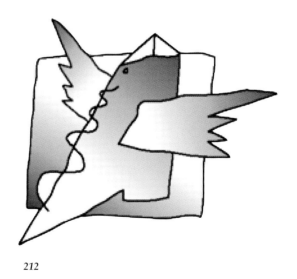

212

213
designer Dana Lamb
design firm Sleepy Hollow Design
client Bikini Shark
Logo for start-up company
for beachwear.

214
designer Mary Anne Mastandrea
design firm Mastandrea Design
client Marine Mammal Center
Logo for the Marine Mammal
Center's 20th anniversary.

215
designer Carol Gravelle
art directors Carol Gravelle
Barbara Mizuno
design firm Mizuno & Associates
client Innovation Sports
Logo showing durability and
toughness of bike trailers.

216
designer Miguel Perez
design firm Mires Design
client AlliKat Records and Cafe
Logo for a record store with a
coffee shop.

217
designer Diane Kuntz
art director Marnell Jameson
design firm Diane Kuntz Design
client Hidden Valley Ranch
Logo for a working ranch in
Calabasas that breeds race horses.

218
designer Ron Miriello
illustrator Tracy Sabin
design firm Miriello Grafico, Inc.
client Browndeer Press
Logo for a children's book
publisher.

213

214

215

216

217

BROWNDEER
PRESS

218

219

designer	Mary Anne Mastandrea
art director	Elizabeth Keenan
design firm	Studio 77/Goldberg Moser O'Neill
client	Heavenly Ski Resort
	Logo for the ski resort's cantina

220

designer	Michael Ketz
illustrator	Laura Jose
design firm	Hetz Advertising & Design
client	Pelican Ridge
	Logo for a real estate housing development.

221

designer	Laurel Bigley Mathe
art director	Paul Page
design firm	Page Design, Inc.
client	NorthBay Healthcare System
	Logo created to promote an event for anyone who had been born at NorthBay Hospital.

222

designer	Cheryl Pelly
design firm	Pelly Design Associates
client	Indigo Iguana
	Logo for a restaurant/cantina.

223

designers	Larry Vigon
	Brian Jackson
illustrator	Daniel and Louise Schriede
design firm	Vigon/Ellis
client	Robin Sloan
	Logo for Robin Sloan's home.

224

designer	Russell Leong
illustrator	Sandy Gin
design firm	Russell Leong Design
client	Radical Concepts
	Logo for custom beanbag chair designers and manufacturers.

219

220

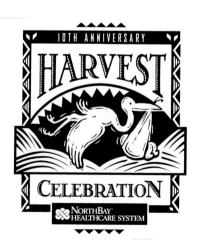

221

222

223   *R o b i n   S l o a n*

224

225
designer Mark Kawakami
design firm M-Studios
client Dog Eat Dog Apparel
Logo for a clothing manufacturer.

226
designer Zion Wu-Yip
art director Jeff Ivarson
illustrator Filip Yip
design firm Ivarson Design Group
client California Graphics, Inc.
Logo for a one-stop digital pre-press service bureau.

227
designers Laura Greer
Darryl Glass
art director Lauren Bruhn
illustrator Ryoichi Yotsumoto
design firm Laura Coe Design Associates
client Titleist and Foot-Joy Worldwide
Logo for a line of kids' golf clubs.

228
designers Larry Vigon
Brian Jackson
illustrator Julie Dennis
design firm Vigon/Ellis
client Total Multimedia
Logo for a fractal compression technology company.

229
designers Ray Wood
Sabine Desmond
design firm Bright Strategic Design
client Mandalay Pictures
Logo for a movie and entertainment company.

225

California Graphics, Inc.

226

227

228

229

230
designer   Jeff Heesch
art director   Michael Stinson
design firm   Stinson Design
client   Viking Star Enterprise
                 Logo for a business consultant.

231
designer   Glenn Martinez
design firm   Glenn Martinez and Associates
client   Enchanté
                 Logo for a producer of books,
                 videos and films geared at boosting
                 children's self-esteem.

232
designer   Jeni Olsen
art director   Nancy Daniels
design firm   The GNU Group
client   Lorin
                 Logo for a hotel based in Indonesia.

233
designer   Daren L. Passolt
design firm   Visualizer Design Studios
client   The Fly
                 Created for a boys' and men's
                 fishing event.

234
designer   José A. Serrano
illustrator   Tracy Sabin
design firm   Mires Design
client   Chaos Lures
                 Logo for fishing lures.

230

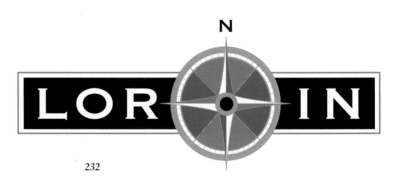

231

Enchanté
LTD

232

233

234

235
designer Jann Bielenberg
design firm Bielenberg Design Group
client Shores Financial
Logo for financial planning
services.

236
designer Steven Morris
design firm Steven Morris Design
client Lolo Company
Logo for toy, gift and game makers.

237
designer Miguel Perez
art director John Ball
illustrator Tracy Sabin
design firm Mires Design
client Rubio's Restaurants
Logo for a low-fat Mexican menu.

238
designer John Ball
illustrator Tracy Sabin
design firm Mires Design
client S.D. Johnson Co.
Logo for a line of fishing products.

239
designer Margo Chase
design firm Margo Chase Design
client Alternative Pick Creative Directory
Section title for "The Alternative
Pick," a creative talent sourcebook
for the music and entertainment
industries.

235

236

237

238

239

240
designer	Glenn Sakamoto
art director	Rod Dyer
design firm	Dyer/Mutchnick Group Inc.
client	Farrier's Nature

Logo for company's environmental television personality.

241
designer	Dickson A. Keyser
design firm	Design Services of Dickson A. Keyser
client	Java Mania

Logo for a coffee house.

242
designer	Bradley W. Grose
design firm	Bradley Grose Design
client	International Church of the Foursquare Gospel

Logo for a gospel record company.

243
designers	Larry Vigon
	Brian Jackson
design firm	Vigon/Ellis
client	Headspace

Logo for a multimedia music provider.

244
designers	Larry Vigon
	Brian Jackson
design firm	Vigon/Ellis
client	E2

Logo for an environmental education program used in the Los Angeles school system.

245
designers	Larry Vigon
	Marc Yeh
design firm	Vigon/Ellis
client	Baldwin Productionsn

Logo for a film production company.

240

241

242

H E A D S P A C E

243

E2
ENVIRONMENT
EDUCATION

244

BALDWIN
PRODUCTIONS

245

246

designer	Barbara D. Cummings
art director	David Parker
design firm	B.D. Cummings/Illustration
client	Vino Desert Classic

Logo for a golf tournament.

247

designer	Lisa Capriotti
design firm	Shurtz/Capriotti
client	Villa Italia

Logo for importer and distributor of fine wines, predominately Italian.

248

designers	Dickson A. Keyser
	Mike Cotsifas
design firm	Cotsifas/Keyser Design Services
client	Bay Area Wine Storage

Logo for the custom storage of collectable wine.

249

designer	Anna Wong
design firm	Akagi Remington
client	Sonoma County Harvest Fair

Logo for region's harvest, showcasing wine, food and crafts.

250

designer	Joyce Sun
art directors	Greg Berman
	Peter Sargent
design firm	Sargent & Berman
client	Cystic Fibrosis

Logo for a fund-raising event benefiting Cystic Fibrosis.

246

247

248

249

A Culinary Evening
with the California
Winemasters
BENEFITING CYSTIC FIBROSIS

250

ALADDIN

251

251
designer   Glenn Martinez
design firm   Glenn Martinez and Associates
client   Aladdin Mortgage
            Logo for a mortgage broker.

252
designer   Alexander Atkins
design firm   Alexander Atkins Design, Inc.
client   Skinny Sippin
            Logo for upscale fruit juice retailer.

253
designer   Michael Ketz
illustrator   Fiona King
design firm   Hetz Advertising & Design
client   Fairway Oaks
            Logo for a real estate housing
            development.

254
designers   Dorothy Remington
            Karin Myint
design firm   Akagi Remington
client   Emily Sagar
            Logo for a caterer and private chef.

252

253

254

255
designer | Rod Dyer
design firm | Dyer/Mutchnick Group Inc.
client | Cheers London Bar & Grill
Logo for this bar is directly related to the one in the television series. This is an adaptation of the original Cheers logo.

256
designer | Arne Ratermanis
design firm | Lorenz Advertising & Design, Inc.
client | Golden Strand Pasta
Logo for a line of pasta products.

257
designers | Rod Dyer
| Terry Song
design firm | Dyer/Mutchnick Group Inc.
client | Sandro's Ciabatta
Logo for a traditional Italian bakery.

258
designer | Steve Twigger
art director | Rod Dyer
design firm | Dyer/Mutchnick Group Inc.
client | Shorty's Diner
Logo for Bruce Willis's restaurant in Haley, Idaho.

255

256

257

258

259
designer   Michael Ketz
illustrator   Dasha Jensen
design firm   Hetz Advertising & Design
client   Pizza Nova
Logo for a restaurant.

260
designer   Mary Anne Mastandrea
art director   Elizabeth Keenan
design firm   Studio 77/Goldberg Moser O'Neill
client   Heavenly Ski Resort
Logo for the ski resort's restaurant.

261
designers   Mike Brower
    Scott Mires
illustrator   Tracy Sabin
design firm   Mires Design
client   Food Group
Logo for a Boyd's Coffee promotion.

262
designers   Scott Mires
    Miguel Perez
art director   John Ball
design firm   Mires Design
client   Taco Pronto
Logo for a Mexican fast-food
restaurant.

259

SLICE OF HEAVEN
Pizza & Pasta

260

261

262

263
designer   Russell Leong
illustrator   Chad Kubo
design firm   Russell Leong Design
client   Roti
                Logo for a rotisserie and grill
                restaurant.

264
designer   Lewis Harrison
design firm   Lewis Harrison Design, Inc.
client   California Produce
                Logo for a wholesale produce
                company marketing to restaurants.

265
designer   Suzanne Bastear
illustrator   Janet Hekking
design firm   Armstrong Associates
client   Sonoma Food & Wine Classic
                Logo for a regional gourmet food
                and fine wine event.

266
designer   Cheri Knoy
art director Karina Lorenz
design firm   Lorenz Advertising & Design, Inc.
client   Topit
                Logo for a product which is a plant
                growth regulator.

267
designer   Jeff Samaripa
design firm   Mires Design
client   Del Mar County Fair
                Logo contest entry for
                Del Mar County Fair.

263

264

265 SONOMA FOOD AND WINE CLASSIC

266

267

268
designer   Becca Smidt
art director Sam Smidt
design firm   Sam Smidt Inc.
client   Spectrum Eye Physicians
              Logo for an eye care business.

269
designer   Howie Idelson
design firm   Urban Image Studio
client   Speed King Racing

270
designer   Konrad Bright
design firm   Bright Strategic Design
client   Panik Productions
              Logo for a film director.

271
designer   Russell Leong
design firm   Russell Leong Design
client   Programmers Press
              Logo for a publisher of
              computer books.

272
designer   Peter Sargent
art director Greg Berman
design firm   Sargent & Berman
client   Toolbox
              Logo for a special effects and
              animation company.

273
designer   Darlene McElroy
design firm   Darlene McElroy Design
client   Four Women Artists
              Logo for four women artists who
              promote themselves as a team and
              have shows together.

274
designer   Jeff Kahn
design firm   Kahn Design
client   The Comedy Coach
              Logo for stand-up comedy trainer
              Neil Leiberman, San Francisco.

268

269

270

271

272

273

274

275
designer Riki Komachi
design firm Riki Komachi
client Architects for Shelter
Logo for the playhouse project.

276
designer Greg Lindy
art directors Jeri Heiden
Michael Rey
design firm Rey International
client Warner Bros. Archives
Logo for the recording company's
classic recordings, reissues and
compilations.

277
designer Ray Marshall
design firm Ray Marshall Design
client John Murray Productions
Logo for an event design and
production company.

278
designer Mark Allen
art director Scott Pryor
design firm Mark Allen Design
client Borders Books
Logos for Borders Book
advertisements.

279
designer Bill Corridori
art director Keith Bright
design firm Bright Strategic Design
client Teenage Website
Logo for the world's first online
fan magazine.

280
designers Leo Terrazas
Daniel Ko
art director Kathy Kirata
illustrator Karen Nakatani
design firm Patrick SooHoo Designers
client L.A. Care Health Plan
Logo for a health care plan to
serve Medi-Cal beneficiaries in
Los Angeles County.

275

276

277

278

279

280

281

designer	Becca Smidt
art director	Sam Smidt
design firm	Sam Smidt, Inc.
client	Women's Community Medical Center

Logo for a friendly, safe and private community medical center for women.

282

designer	Han Vu
art director	Jeffrey Shurtz
design firm	Shurtz/Capriotti
client	Sybase Worldwide Customer Support & Services

Logo for a database software company

283

designer	Christine Cava
client	Log On America

Logo for an online internet service.

284

designer	Gale Spitzley
art director	José A. Serrano
illustrator	Dan Thoner
design firm	Mires Design
client	Pannikin

Logo for a 25th Anniversary promotion.

285

designer	Deborah Hom
art director	John Ball
design firm	Mires Design
client	Fusion Media

Logo for a multimedia developer.

286

designer	Dickson A. Keyser
design firm	Design Services of Dickson A. Keyser
client	Self Identity

Logo for designer who specializes in solving people's identity problems.

287

designers	Steve Turner
	Paul Weingartner
art director	Joan Hausman
design firm	Hausman Design
client	Meris Laboratories, Inc.

Logo for a testing laboratory.

281

282

Log On America

283

284

285

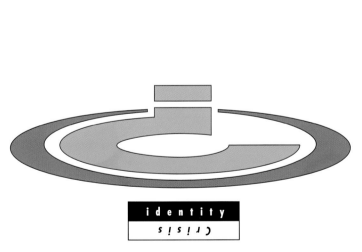

286

287 MERIS

288
designer   Mario Porto
art director   Lisa Capriotti
design firm   Shurtz/Capriotti
client   Made to Order Memories
Logo for upscale custom
made gifts.

289
designer   Han Vu
art director   Jeffrey Shurtz
design firm   Shurtz/Capriotti
client   Sybase Training Program
Logo for a database software
company.

290
designer   Shelly Weir-Martinez
art director   Jeffrey Shurtz
design firm   Shurtz/Capriotti
client   San Francisco Youth At Risk
Logo for a non-profit organization
that helps disadvantaged children
get education and jobs.

291
designer   Mike Brower
illustrator   Tracy Sabin
design firm   Mires Design
client   MG Swing Company
Logo for a painting contractor
specializing in faux.

292
designer   Deborah Hom
art director   Scott Mires
illustrator   Tracy Sabin
design firm   Mires Design
client   Harcourt Brace & Co.
Logo for a T-shirt commemorating
completion of a series of
educational text books for children.

288

289

290

SINCE ★ 1993
M.G. SWING COMPANY
Painting Contractors

291

Bookworms
HARCOURT BRACE & CO.

292

293
designer   Russell Leong
design firm   Russell Leong Design
client   City of Palo Alto Parks &
Recreation
Logo for Palo Alto's annual black
and white ball.

294
designer   Dickson A. Keyser
design firm   Cotsifas/Keyser Design Services
client   JDM Catering Co.
Logo for a catering company with
an eclectic style.

295
designer   Russell Leong
design firm   Russell Leong Design
client   Richardson Architects
Logo for an architectural firm.

296
designer   Becca Smidt
art director   Sam Smidt
design firm   Sam Smidt Inc.
client   Versaggi Bio-Communications
Logo for a bio-medical
marketing/communications firm.

297
designer   Nita Ybarra
art director   Jeffrey Shurtz
design firm   Shurtz/Capriotti
client   Sun Microsystems
Logo for Sun Ware catalog.

CITY OF PALO ALTO'S

BLACK & WHITE
BALL

293

294

RICHARDSON ■ ▲ ● ⌂ [ARCHITECTS]

295

296   VERSAGGI BIO COMMUNICATIONS

297

298

designer	Calvin Chiu
design firm	Edcal Design
client	Herbert von Karajan Club
	Logo for a classical music conductors club.

299

designer	Martha Newton Furman
design firm	Martha Newton Furman Design & Illustration
client	San José Chamber Orchestra
	Logo for a professional chamber orchestra.

299A

designer	Martha Newton Furman
design firm	Martha Newton Furman Design & Illustration
client	San José State University School of Music & Dance
	Logo for Center for Research in Electro-Acoustic Music.

300

designer	Paul Morales
art director	Robert Kastigar
illustrator	Georgia Deaver
design firm	Halleck Design Group
client	San Jose Symphony
	Logo for the symphony orchestra

301

designer	Joe Miller
design firm	Joe Miller's Company
client	KSJS Public Radio
	Logo for an eclectic music and public affairs radio station.

297

298

299

SAN JOSE SYMPHONY

300

301

302
designer   Rod Dyer
design firm   Dyer/Mutchnick Group Inc.
client   Universal Records
Logo for a record company.

303
designer   Laurie Carrigan
art director   Steve Turner
design firm   Hausman Design
client   IBSS Business Group
Logo for a semi-conductor
manufacturer.

304
designer   Bill Corridori
art director   Keith Bright
design firm   Bright Strategic Design
client   KCET Store of Knowledge
Logo for a retail store selling books,
CD ROMs, etc. on knowledge,
education and creativity
worldwide.

305
designers   José A. Serrano
     Miguel Perez
illustrator   Tracy Sabin
design firm   Mires Design
client   Found Stuff Paper Works
Logo for recycled organically
grown cotton.

306
designer   Steven Morris
design firm   Steven Morris Design
client   Arts al Fresco
Logo for arts, music and
dance festivals.

307
designer   Lewis Harrison
illustrator   Patrice Roberts
design firm   Lewis Harrison Design, Inc.
client   Cibacs
Logo for an educational program
for international and
communication studies.

302

303

304

305

306

307

308
designer — Mary Anne Mastandrea
art director — Elizabeth Keenan
design firm — Mastandrea Design
client — Heavenly Ski Resort
Logo for the ski resort's 40th anniversary.

309
designer — José A. Serrano
illustrator — Tracy Sabin
design firm — Mires Design
client — Deleo Clay Tile Company
Logo for a new line of clay tiles to be sold in Hawaii.

310
designer — Julia Becker Foug
art director — Lisa Capriotti
design firm — Shurtz/Capriotti
client — Beaver Creek Lodge
Logo for a bistro/restaurant in Colorado, USA.

311
designer — Paul Weingartner
design firm — pw Design
client — California Primary Care Association
Logo for a non-profit medical association.

312
designer — Mike Cotsifas
design firm — Cotsifas/Keyser Design Services
client — Boulders Golf Center
Logo for a golf driving range.

313
designer — Daren L. Passolt
design firm — Visualizer Design Studios
client — Molokai Magic
Logo for maker of custom stained glass art and windows.

314
designer — Daren L. Passolt
design firm — Visualizer Design Studios
client — Mystic Mountain
Logo created for an all natural hand made soap company.

315
designer — Barbara Brown
design firm — Barbara Brown Marketing and Design
client — Channel Islands Properties
Logo for Channel Islands Properties reflecting a local natural landmark.

308

309

310

311

312

313

314

315

316
designer   Diane Kuntz
dillustrator   Linda Eberle
design firm   Diane Kuntz Design
client   UniHealth
Logo for a corporate health care
management program.

317
designers   Dorothy Remington
           Joanna Wiraatmadja
art director   Doug Akagi
design firm   Akagi Remington
client   Hacienda Corazon
Logo for a high-end residential
community in the Philippines.

318
designer   Jeff Kahn
design firm   Kahn Design
client   Honey Rose Baking Co.
Logo for a health food bakery.

319
designers   Larry Vigon
           Brian Jackson
design firm   Vigon/Ellis
client   Elixir
Logo for a Chinese herbal
remedy store.

320
designer   Ray Wood
art director   Keith Bright
design firm   Bright Strategic Design
client   California Community Foundation
Logo for a foundation to raise and
distribute funds to worthy causes
and institutions.

321
designer   Ray Wood
art director   Keith Bright
design firm   Bright Strategic Design
client   The State of California
Environmental Protection Agency
Logo for agency protecting the
environment.

322
designer   Daren L. Passolt
design firm   Visualizer Design Studios
client   Cloverleaf Pre Schools
Logo created for Cloverleaf
Private Pre Schools.

316

317

318

elixir

Tonics & Teas

319

CALIFORNIA
COMMUNITY
FOUNDATION

320

Cal / EPA

321

Cloverleaf Pre Schools

322

323
designer   Jeff Ivarson
design firm   Ivarson Design Group
client   Fenwick Willow
          Logo for a manufacturer of high
          quality fishing rods.

324
designer   Ramsey Said
art director   Jeff Ivarson
illustrator   Chet Phillips
design firm   Ivarson Design Group
client   3M Pharmaceutical
          Logo for Zartra
          pharmaceutical creme.

325
designer   Jill Thayer
design firm   Jill Thayer Associates
client   Rio Bravo Resort
          Logo for a resort located in the
          Southern Sierras.

326
designer   Qris Yamashita
art director   Rod Dyer
design firm   Dyer/Mutchnick Group Inc.
client   Evergreen Entertainment
          Logo for a Hallmark Film
          Production Company.

327
designer   Joe Miller
design firm   Joe Miller's Company
client   Shade
          Logo for an etherial rock group.

328
designer   Glenn Johnson
art director   Jerry Takigawa
design firm   Jerry Takigawa Design
client   Natural Selection Foods
          Logo for growers and
          marketers of specialty
          salads and organic
          vegetables.

329
designer   Paul Weingartner
design firm   pw Design
client   Settimana Fiorentina
          Logo for a festival
          of Italian culture.

W I L L O W

323

324

An Extraordinary Resort

325

326

327

NATURAL SELECTION FOODS

328

SETTIMANA FIORENTINA

329

330
designer   Ron Miriello
illustrator   Michelle Aranda
design firm   Miriello Grafico, Inc.
client   Tomato's
               Logo for an Italian restaurant.

331
designer   Qris Yamashita
art director   Rod Dyer
design firm   Dyer/Mutchnick Group Inc.
client   Cafe America
               Logo for a restaurant.

332
designer   John Ball
illustrator   Nadeem Zzidi
design firm   Mires Design
client   Woodstock Idea Factory
               Logo for a creative consultant.

333
designer   Joe Miller
art director   Mai Nguyen, Quantum
design firm   Joe Miller's Company
client   Fireball
               Logo for a disk drive manufacturer.

334
designer   Linda Kahn
art director   Micki Wilson
design firm   Frank Templeton Inc.
client   Micki Wilson/Franklin
               Templeton Inc.
               Logo for a new software program
               to access clients' accounts.

335
designer   Debbie Smith
art director   Leila Daubert
design firm   Addis Group
client   Compton's Home Library
               Logo for a software business.

330

331

332

333

334

335

DISNEYLAND GRAD 95 NITE

336

336

designer	Barbara Bettis
art director	John Hamagami
design firm	Hamagami/Carroll & Associates
client	Disneyland Grad Nite 1995
	Logo for graduating high school
	seniors program.

337

designer	Mary Anne Mastandrea
art director	Elizabeth Keenan
design firm	Studio 77/Goldberg Moser O'Neill
client	Number Nine
	Logo for a high-tech company..

338

designer	Barbara Bettis
art director	John Hamagami
design firm	Hamagami/Carroll & Associates
client	Disneyland Grad Nite 1994
	Logo for graduating high school
	seniors program.

339

designer	Paula Sugarman
illustrator	Brad Maur
design firm	Page Design, Inc.
client	KVIE
	Logo for Channel 6 public
	television station.

337

338

339

340
designers　Doyle Harrison
　　　　　Mary Evelyn McGough
art director　Mike Salisbury
design firm　Mike Salisbury
　　　　　Communications, Inc.
client　　Gamers
　　　　　Logo for online internet gaming.

341
designer　Mary Evelyn McGough
art director　Mike Salisbury
design firm　Mike Salisbury
　　　　　Communications, Inc.
client　　Rage
　　　　　Logo for a magazine.

342
designer　Margo Chase
design firm　Margo Chase Design
client　　Westland Graphics
　　　　　"May" logo for a promotional
　　　　　calendar.

343
designer　Kenneth Lewis
design firm　Kenneth Lewis Design
client　　Leo Gong Photography
　　　　　Logo for a photography studio.

344
art director　Patti Judd
design firm　Juddesign
client　　Seating Concepts
　　　　　Logo for an international theater
　　　　　seating manufacturer.

345
designer　Jon Lagda
art director　Ron Scheibel
design firm　Hunt, Rook & Scheibel
client　　Moss Micro
　　　　　Logo for a software
　　　　　engineering company.

346
designer　Barbara Bettis
art director　Justin Carroll
design firm　Hamagami/Carroll & Associates
client　　20th Century Fox
　　　　　Logo for "The X Files"
　　　　　television program.

340

341

342

343

344

345

MOSS MICRO

346

347
designer   Russell Leong
design firm   Russell Leong Design
client   E3
                Logo for a manufacturer of digital
                sampling keyboards.

348
designer   Amy Williams
art director   Patti Judd
design firm   Juddesign
client   The Dakota Group
                Logo for a film and video
                production company.

349
designer   Mary Anne Mastandrea
design firm   Mastandrea Design
client   Mastandrea Design
                Logo for the design firm.

350
designer   Rod Dyer
design firm   Dyer/Mutchnick Group Inc.
client   Leo Burnett/Sony
                Retail logo for Sony
                Maximum Television.

351
designer   Martha Newton Furman
design firm   Martha Newton Furman Design &
                Illustration
client   Theresa Vargo Photography
                Logo for photographer
                Theresa Vargo.

352
designer   Russell Leong
illustrator   Meredith Chew
design firm   Russell Leong Design
client   Exponential
                Logo for a manufacturer of
                computer chips.

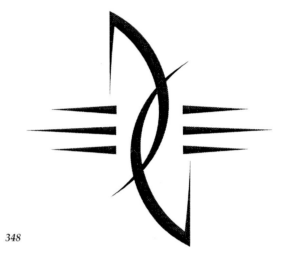

347

348

MASTANDREA · DESIGN

349

SURROUND SOUND™

350

351

352

353

354

353
designer   Peter Sargent
art director   Peter Sargent
design firm   Sargent & Berman
client   Advanced Travel Management
Logo for a travel agency.

354
designer   Glenn Sakamoto
art director   Rod Dyer
design firm   Dyer/Mutchnick Group Inc.
client   Players Network
Logo for a Las Vegas
television network.

355
designer   Qris Yamashita
art director   Rod Dyer
design firm   Dyer/Mutchnick Group Inc.
client   O'Melveny & Myers LLP
Logo for a law firm.

356
designer   Peter Cook
design firm   Dyer/Mutchnick Group Inc.
client   Gramercy Pictures
Logo for a motion picture company.

357
designer   Rod Dyer
design firm   Dyer/Mutchnick Group Inc.
client   Bregman/Baer Productions, Inc.
Logo for a motion picture
production company.

355

356

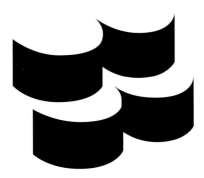

357

358
designer	Jamie Graupner
art director	John White
design firm	White Design, Inc.
client	Barrington Consulting Group

Logo for legal consultants for business and engineering.

359
designer	Glenn Sakamoto
art director	Rod Dyer
design firm	Dyer/Mutchnick Group Inc.
client	Ironhawk Design Co.

Logo for an ironwork artisan.

360
designer	Greg Lindy
design firm	Rey International
client	AMP

Logo for a magazine-like website for MCA records.

361
designer	Gregory Thomas
design firm	Gregory Thomas Associates
client	Walden Partners

Logo for a designer and manufacturer of pop displays for Fortune 500 companies.

362
designer	Hun Wynn
art director	Rod Dyer
design firm	Dyer/Mutchnick Group Inc.
client	Abrams Artists Agency

Logo for a creative talent agency.

363
designers	Jennifer Morla
	Craig Bailey
design firm	Morla Design
client	San Francisco Production Group

Logo for a video production facility specializing in animation, sound and film.

358

359

360

WALDEN PARTNERS

361

ABRAMS ARTISTS AGENCY

362

363

364
designer   Daren L. Passolt
design firm Visualizer Design Studios
client   Tactic
             Logo for a database software
             company.

365
designer   Daren L. Passolt
design firm Visualizer Design Studios
client   Integrated Facilities Resources
             Corporate identity created for an
             internally operated facilities
             solution provider.

366
designer   Daren L. Passolt
design firm Visualizer Design Studios
client   Apple Computer, Inc.
             Created for a product support
             booklet for Latin American and the
             Caribbean marketplace.

367
designer   Brad Maur
art director Paul Page
design firm   Page Design, Inc.
client   Reebok
              Logo for a Reebok-sponsored
              expedition to climb the Mt K2 on
              the North Ridge.

368
designer   Daren L. Passolt
design firm Visualizer Design Studios
client   Rhetorex
             Tapi Express logo created for a
             voice activated software package.

369
designers   Larry Vigon
             Marc Yeh
illustrator Marc Yeh
design firm Vigon/Ellis
client   Matinee Entertainment
             Logo for an animation production
             company.

364

365

366

367

368

369

matinee
ENTERTAINMENT

370 # LOS ANGELES

371

372

A C I ™

WORLDWIDE DISTRIBUTION

370
designer — Taleen Bedikian
art director — Ray Wood
design firm — Bright Strategic Design
client — Los Angeles Convention &
Visitors Bureau
Logo designed to bring visitors and
conventions to Los Angeles.

371
designer — William Kent
art director — Tricia Rauen
design firm — Buz Design Group
client — Adelson Entertainment
Logo for entertainment
productions.

372
designers — Jann Bielenberg
Lea Horrmitz
design firm — Bielenberg Design Group
client — ACI
Logo for a film distribution
company.

373
designer — Darlene McElroy
design firm — Darlene McElroy Design
client — Darlene McElroy Design
Logo for a design studio.

374
designer — Darlene McElroy
design firm — Darlene McElroy Design
client — Maria Piscopo
Logo for an artists and
photographers representative and
art consultant.

375
designer — Gina Simpson
design firm — Sexton/Simpson Design
client — Miller Construction
Logo for a construction company.

373

374

375

376
designer	Ray Wood
art director	Keith Bright
design firm	Bright Strategic Design
client	Mercury Wave Craft

Logo for manufacturers of a new jet ski.

377
designer	Ray Wood
art director	Keith Bright
design firm	Bright Strategic Design
client	Bullwhackers

Logo for a casino and entertainment center.

378
designer	Mamoru Shimokochi
art director	Anne Reeves
design firm	Shimokochi/Reeves
client	Kagoshima

Proposed logo for the prefecture of Japan.

379
designer	Mark Allen
art director	Cynthia Kinney
design firm	Mark Allen Design
client	Justice Records

Logo for a tribute CD for Willie Nelson.

380
designers	Dorothy Remington
	Amelie Von Fluegge
illustrator	Amelie Von Fluegge
design firm	Akagi Remington
client	Remington Design

Logo for a graphic design studio. Initials stand for Dorothy Remington and Remington Design.

381
designer	Jeff Heesch
art director	Michael Stinson
design firm	Stinson Design
client	Jennifer and Jeffrey Heesch

Logo for the Heesch's wedding.

376

377

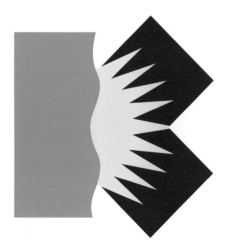

378

379

380

381

382
designer   Mark Kawakami
design firm M-Studios
client   Honda
Logo for an automotive
manufacturer.

383
designers   Larry Vigon
           Brian Jackson
design firm Vigon/Ellis
client   Julie Dennis
Logo for a photographer.

384
designers   Kathryn Thornton
           Laura Mische
art director Linda Warren
design firm Warren Group
client   Creative Wonder
Logo for an event production
company.

385
designer   Barbara D. Cummings
design firm B.D. Cummings/Illustration
client   DAA
Logo for a full-service
advertising agency.

386
designer   Gordon Mortensen
illustrator   John Bleck
design firm Mortensen Design
client   Rendition
Logo for high-speed texture
wrapping and 3-D rendering for
animation on PCs.

387
designer   Dickson A. Keyser
design firm Design Services of Dickson A.
           Keyser
client   Weaver Surfboards
Logo for a surfboard shaper.

388
designer   Jeffry Burne
design firm Burne Design
client   Paramount Fasteners
Logo for a distributor of bolts, nuts,
screws and other fasteners.

382

383   J U L I E   D E N N I S

384

385

rendition

386

387

PARAMOUNT FASTENERS

388

389
designer   Paul Morales
design firm   Onyx Design Inc.
client   Double Hull Tankers Ltd.
Logo for a double hull tanker
consultant.

390
designer   Mark Kawakami
design firm   M-Studios
client   Cru Clothing
Logo for a sports apparel company

391
designer   Howie Idelson
design firm   Urban Image Studio
client   Pacific Athletic Club

392
designers   Larry Vigon
Brian Jackson
design firm   Vigon/Ellis
client   If..
Logo for high tech database
products.

393
designers   Larry Vigon
Brian Jackson
design firm   Vigon/Ellis
client   Vigon/Ellis
Logo for a brand development and
graphic design group.

394
designer   Kim Sage
art director   Petrula Vrontikis
design firm   Vrontikis Design Office
client   Playpen
Logo for film and television
motion graphics.

395
designer   Paula Sugarman
design firm   Page Design, Inc.
client   Zellerbach Paper
Logo for a paper merchant's paper
specification service for the
design industry.

389

390

391

392

393

394

CLUB

395

396
designer   Becca Smidt
design firm Becca Smidt
client   Googie Tours
             Logo for a company giving tours of
             historical 1950s coffee shops,
             diners and bowling alleys in L.A.

397
designer   Becca Smidt
art director Sam Smidt
design firm Sam Smidt Inc.
client   Turner Martin
             Logo for a gift store selling hand
             made objects for the home.

398
designer   Jann Bielenberg
illustrator Eric David
design firm Bielenberg Design Group
client   The Cassie Awards
             Logo for telecast awards show for
             excellence in the casino/
             resort entertainment industry.

399
designer   Mark Allen
art director Jon Sparrman
design firm Mark Allen Design
client   Warner Bros.
             Logo for a proposed movie title.

400
designer   Howie Idelson
design firm Urban Image Studio
client   Style Kings Clothing

401
designer   Mark Allen
art director Bernie Urban
design firm Mark Allen Design
client   Marketing Foundations/
             Superior Coffee and Foods
             Logo for a coffee brand.

396

397

398

399

U.S.A. Quality

400

Signatures

401

402
designer	Howie Idelson
design firm	Urban Image Studio
client	Pacific Athletic Club

403
designer	Howie Idelson
design firm	Urban Image Studio
client	Zen Bakery

404
designer	Howie Idelson
design firm	Urban Image Studio
client	Western Jeans

405
designer	Howie Idelson
design firm	Urban Image Studio
client	Pro Circuit

406
designer	Howie Idelson
design firm	Urban Image Studio
client	Gearbox/Renspeed
	Logo for motorsport accessories

407
designer	Howie Idelson
design firm	Urban Image Studio
client	Western Jeans

408
designer	Howie Idelson
design firm	Urban Image Studio
client	Malibu Boardriders Club

402

403

404

405

RENSPEED

406

407

408

409
designer | Mark Allen
| Harrison Allen
art director | Gail Harrison
design firm | Mark Allen Design
client | Hanna-Barbera
| Logo for the 60th anniversary of
| "The Wizard of Oz."

410
designer | Mark Allen
art director | Matti Leshem
design firm | Mark Allen Design
client | S.C. Headline News
| Web site logo for
| "The Second City."

411
designer | Mark Allen
art director | Laurel Buerk
design firm | Mark Allen Design
client | Outdoor Recreation Group/Oblique
| Logo for Snowboard merchandise.

412
designer | Mark Allen
art directors | Stacie Seifrit
| Ann Wilkins
design firm | Mark Allen Design
client | KROQ
| Logo for a radio station talk show.

413
designer | Lisa Capriotti
design firm | Shurtz/Capriotti
client | Wells Fargo
| Logo for in-house use for approval
| on in-branch materials.

414
designer | Lisa Capriotti
illustrator | Dave Danz
design firm | Shurtz/Capriotti
client | Wells Fargo Bank
| Logo for an employee
| communications newsletter.

409

410

411

412

413

414

415
designer   Mark Allen
art director   Bill Leissring
design firm   Mark Allen Design
client   Miller Beer
                  Logo for an advertising campaign.

416
designer   Han Vu
art director   Jeffrey Shurtz
design firm   Shurtz/Capriotti
client   Hirsch Enterprises
                  Logo for a trade show event with a
                  Mexican theme.

417
designer   John Ball
illustrator   Tracy Sabin
design firm   Mires Design
client   California Center For The Arts
                  Logo for an event at the arts center.

418
designer   Michael Cotsifas
art director   Marc Eis
design firm   Shugart Matson Marketing
                  Communications
client   VISX
                  Logo for a manufacturer of lasers
                  for vision correction.

419
designer   Dickson A. Keyser
design firm   Design Services of Dickson A.
                  Keyser
client   Trash
                  Logo for a company making gifts
                  from recycled products.

420
designer   Mark Allen
art director   Dave Parmley
design firm   Mark Allen Design
client   I-Storm
                  Logo for a website design
                  company.

415

416

417

418

419

420

421
designers   John Ball
                Gale Spitzley
design firm Mires Design
client   California Center For The Arts
                Logo for an exhibition of animal-inspired artworks.

422
designers   Deborah Hom
                Scott Mires
illustrator Tracy Sabin
design firm Mires Design
client   Ear To Ear
                Logo for a music production/composing house.

423
designer   Miguel Perez
art director John Ball
design firm Mires Design
client   California Center For The Arts
                Logo for a multi-disciplinary regional arts center.

424
designer   Mike Brower
art director Scott Mires
illustrator Tracy Sabin
design firm Mires Design
client   Food Group
                Logo for a point of purchase poster to promote a new blended shake for Boyd's Coffee.

425
designer   Miguel Perez
art director José A. Serrano
design firm Mires Design
client   Donnelley Enterprise Solutions
                Logo for a company that provides integrated information management services.

421

422

423

424

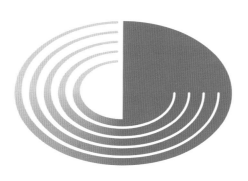

DONNELLEY ENTERPRISE SOLUTIONS

INCORPORATED

425

426
designer   Mark Kawakami
design firm M-Studios
client   Airtight
Logo for a wetsuit manufacturer.

427
designer   Tracy E. Moon
design firm Aerial
client   PC.IABP
Logo for personal computer/
medical equipment interface
software.

428
designer   Mark Allen
design firm Mark Allen Design
client   Chris Reade Communications
Logo for rep. who represents New
York rap groups.

429
designer   José A. Serrano
illustrator Tracy Sabin
design firm Mires Design
client   Chingones
Logo for custom street wear.

430
designer   José A. Serrano
illustrator Tracy Sabin
design firm Mires Design
client   Magic Carpet Books
Logo for a classic fantasy literature
book series.

431
designer   José A. Serrano
illustrator Carl Vanderschuit
design firm Mires Design
client   Agassi Enterprises
Logo for a new gripping powder.

426

427

428

429

MAGIC
CARPET

BOOKS

430

FUSION

431

432
designer   Tracy E. Moon
design firm   Aerial
client   Impact Unlimited
Logo for exhibit and event design
and marketing services.

433
designer   Tracy E. Moon
design firm   Aerial
client   Lenox Roomn
Logo for an upscale, upper east
side Manhattan restaurant.

434
designer   Tracy E. Moon
design firm   Aerial
client   Datascope
Logo for a leader in innovative
tools, technology and equipment
for the healthcare industry.

435
designer   Tracy E. Moon
design firm   Aerial
client   Idiom
Logo for a strategic naming firm.

436
designer   Tracy E. Moon
design firm   Aerial
client   Beach House
Logo for a seaside hotel/
condominium development.

437
designer   Tracy E. Moon
design firm   Aerial
client   Phoenix Network
Logo for telecommunications
billing services.

432

LENOX ROOM

433

Datascope

434

id´i·om

435

Beach House

436

PhoenixNetwork.

437

438
designer   Tracy E. Moon
design firm   Aerial
client   ACA JOE
Logo for men's casual clothing.

439
designer   Tracy E. Moon
illustrator   John Mattos
design firm   Aerial
client   Hotel Bohéme
Logo for a hotel/hospitality industry.

440
designer   Steven Morris
design firm   Steven Morris Design
client   RPM Color
Logo for a color scanning, film
output service bureau.

441
designer   Miguel Perez
art director   John Ball
design firm   Mires Design
client   Copeland Reis Talent Agency
Logo for a talent agency.

442
designer   Pilar Dowell
art director   Pilar Dowell
design firm   Dowell Design
client   Intenational Hapkido Karate
Association
Logo for a Karate Association.

443
designer   Tracy E. Moon
design firm   Aerial
client   Calypso Imaging
Logo for a digital color lab.

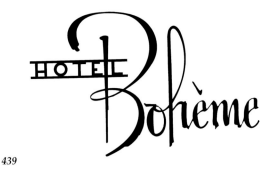

438

439

440

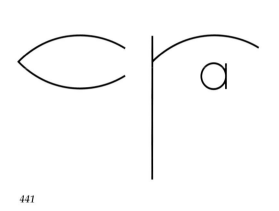

441

INTERNATIONAL

442

H A P K I D O
K A R A T E
A S S O C I A T I O N®

443

444
designer	Maria Wang-Horn
design firm	Wang/Hutner
client	Auctionet
	Logo for a computer hardware auction company on the internet.

445
designer	Thomas Harley Bond
design firm	SBG Partners
client	Hewlett Packard
	Logo for products within Hewlett Packard's Interactive Entertainment Division.

446
designer	John Hopkins
design firm	Hop Art
client	Hop Art
	Logo representing designer's own graphic design studio.

447
designers	Brian Jacobson
	Jeanne Namkung
art director	Thomas McNulty
illustrator	Jeanne Namkung
design firm	Profile Design
client	Mariani Nut Company
	Logo for a grower and processor of raw nuts in California's Central Valley.

448
designer	Lena Tonseth
art director	Kenichi Nishiwaki
design firm	Profile Design
client	San Francisco Opera Guild
	Logo for the guild which supports and promotes education of the arts and raises funds for the San Francisco Opera.

449
designer	Brian Jacobson
art director	Thomas McNulty
illustrator	Liz Wheaton
design firm	Profile Design
client	Dr. McDougall's Right Foods
	Logo for a developer and manufacturer of healthy foods.

444

445

446

447

448

449

450
designer	Howard Ian Schiller
design firm	TL-R & Associates
client	Insite
	Logo for a website marketing and development company.

451
designer	Riki Komachi
design firm	Riki Komachi
client	Venice 5/10 K
	Logo for the Venice 5/10 K run.

452
designer	John Sabel
art director	Rod Dyer
design firm	Dyer/Mutchnick Group Inc.
client	Sensa
	Logo for fresh, new herbal drinks with natural flavors.

453
designer	Qris Yamashita
art director	Rod Dyer
design firm	Dyer/Mutchnick Group Inc.
client	Big Ticket Television
	Logo for comedy programming.

454
designers	Jeanne Namkung
	Anthony Luk
art directors	Kenichi Nishiwaki
	Russell Baker
design firm	Profile Design
client	Project Open Hand
	Logo for a non-profit organization in San Francisco which provides meals, groceries and health servies to people with AIDS.

455
designer	Peter Nam
design firm	Peter Nam Design
client	San Francisco Tea Symposium
	Logo for educational seminars on tea.

450

451

452

453

PROJECT
Open Hand

454

455

456
designer Howard Ian Schiller
design firm Designwise
client Integer Poet Software
Logo for a computer programming
and consulting company.

457
designer Greg Lindy
design firm Rey International
client Lux Typographics
Logo for a type foundry.

458
designer Paul Weingartner
design firm pw Design
client Lulli Ronchi
Logo for an interior design firm.

459
designer Howard Ian Schiller
art director Tony Lane-Roberts
illustrator Wayne Clark
design firm TL-R & Associates
client Rich Animation Studios
Logo for an animation production
company.

460
designers Paul Chock
Chris Gollmer
art director Mark Bergman
design firm SBG Partners
client Picture This Home
Logo for software for computer-
aided program for architects.

461
designer Greg Lindy
art director Michael Rey
design firm Rey International
client Meigneux Kerr Studios
Logo for a photography and
architecture studio.

462
designer Greg Lindy
art directors Tim Stedman
Jonas Livingston
design firm Rey International
client MCA
Logo for music from motion
pictures available on soundtracks
from MCA records.

456

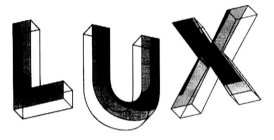

457

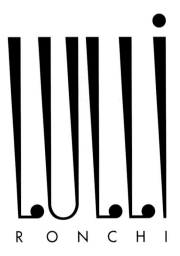

458

459

460

461

462

463
designer	Mark Jones
art directors	Primo Angeli
	Carlo Pagoda
art director	Primo Angeli
client	Wilbur-Ellis Company

Logo for a company specializing in agricultural products for the international market.

464
designers	Jenny Baker
	Mark Jones
art directors	Primo Angeli
	Ron Hoffman
illustrator	Liz Wheaton
design firm	Primo Angeli Inc.
client	Ferris & Roberts

Logo for an herbal line of imported English teas with a perceived established English heritage.

465
designers	Terrence Tong
	Ed Cristman
art directors	Primo Angeli
	Carlo Pagoda
illustrator	Robert Evans
design firm	Primo Angeli Inc.
client	Mariani Packing Company

Logo for a line of dried fruit that reinforces the fresh fruit origins.

466
designer	Bill Corridori
art director	Keith Bright
design firm	Bright Strategic Design
client	Gratis Restaurant

Logo for a gourmet restaurant serving fat-free cuisine.

467
designer	Maria Wang-Horn
design firm	Wang/Hutner Design
client	1st Byte

Logo for a computer hardware auction company on the internet.

468
designer	Maria Wang-Horn
design firm	Wang/Hutner Design
client	Vertigo

Logo for a restaurant and bar.

463

464

465

466

467

RESTAURANT & BAR

468

469

BIRTHMARK PRODUCTIONS

470 the GRAPELINE

471

ACQUARELLO
THE TRAVEL ARTIST

469

designer	Jeni Olsen
design firm	JO Design
client	Green T.V.

Logo for a cable television show which profiles environmentally aware companies and people.

470

designer	Jeni Olsen
design firm	JO Design
client	The Grapeline

Logo for a comany offering computer network installations and software support for retail systems in wineries.

471

designer	Steve Twigger
art director	Rod Dyer
design firm	Dyer/Mutchnick Group Inc.
client	Acquarello

Logo for a travel agent in Italy.

472

designers	Larry Vigon
	Brian Jackson
design firm	Vigon/Ellis
client	Mr. Lucky's

Logo for a restaurant.

473

designer	Glenn Sakamoto
art director	Rod Dyer
design firm	Dyer/Mutchnick Group Inc.
client	Tixa Technology

Logo for a software/hardware company.

472

TIXA TECHNOLOGY

473

474
designer	Sam Lising
art director	Petrula Vrontikis
design firm	Vrontikis Design Office
client	Greenhood & Company
	Logo for new media
	technology experts.

475
designers	Chip Toll
	Judy Radiche
art director	Primo Angeli
design firm	Primo Angeli Inc.
client	Spectrum Foods
	Logo for the Tutto Mare restaurant.

476
designer	Russell Leong
design firm	Russell Leong Design
client	Betelnut
	Logo for a Pan-Asian restaurant.

477
designer	Rod Dyer
design firm	Dyer/Mutchnick Group Inc.
client	Monk Recording Group
	Logo for a cutting edge recording
	company.

478
designer	Chris Cava
art director	Rod Dyer
design firm	Dyer/Mutchnick Group Inc.
client	Fremont Street Experience
	Logo for Fremont Street
	Experience, Las Vegas.

474

475

476

477

478

479
designer   Daren L. Passolt
design firm Visualizer Design Studios
client   Amdahl Corporation
            Logo Created for the
            25th anniversary of Amdahl.

480
designer   Aaron Atchison
art director Tricia Rauen
design firm   Buz Design Group
client   The Loop
              Logo for an internet server.

481
designer   Tracy Titus
art director Paul Page
illustrator   Kimberly Bickel
design firm   Page Design, Inc.
client   TheraCare Rehab
              Logo for a provider of care for
              elderly people through
              rehabilitation.

482
designer   Darlene McElroy
design firm   Darlene McElroy Design
client   Timbuktu
              Logo for a folk and tribal shop.

483
designer   Kelli Kunkle-Day
art director Tricia Rauen
design firm   Buz Design Group
client   Rock Architects
              Logo for an architectural firm.

484
designer   Ron Miriello
design firm   Miriello Grafico, Inc.
client   Lux Kahvé
              Logo for a restaurant/lounge.

479

480

481

482

483

484

485
designers	Larry Vigon
	Marc Yeh
design firm	Vigon/Ellis
client	LAX
	Logo for the Los Angeles Department of Airports renovation project.

486
designers	Larry Vigon
	Marc Yeh
art director	Todo Reublin
illustrator	Michael Elins
design firm	Vigon/Ellis
client	DreamWorks SKG
	Logo for the music division of DreamWorks.

487
designer	Kimberly Bickel
design firm	Page Design, Inc.
client	Amongst Friends
	Logo for a photographer who concentrates on black-and-white portraits and then hand tints them.

488
designer	Daren L. Passolt
design firm	Visualizer Design Studios
client	Rhetorex
	RealCT logo created for a voice activated software program.

489
designer	Cheryl Pelly
design firm	Pelly Design Associates
client	Lock Shock
	Logo for mountain bike shock absorbers.

490
designer	Cheryl Pelly
design firm	Designworks/USA
client	Deere
	Proposed logo for the John Deere industrial tractor division.

485

486

487

488

489

490

491
designers	Philippe Becker
	Rolando Rosler
art director	Primo Angeli
design firm	Primo Angeli Inc.
client	Omnihost
	Logo for worldwide
	communications software.

492
designer	Terrence Tong
art directors	Primo Angeli
	Ron Hoffman
design firm	Primo Angeli Inc.
client	ATEC
	Logo for a sports equipment
	company that specializes in
	baseball training equipment.

493
designer	Brad Maur
design firm	Page Design, Inc.
client	Magnum Gear
	Logo for a manufacturer of outdoor
	and rugged footwear.

494
designers	Primo Angeli
	Ian McClean
art directors	Rolando Rosler
	Mark Crumpacker
design firm	Primo Angeli Inc.
client	Lavazza
	Logo designed for the entry
	of an Italian coffee into the
	American market.

495
designer	Lissa Patrizi
design firm	Patrizi Designs
client	Jeff's Decorative Finishes
	Logo for custom painting and
	art furniture.

496
designers	Daren L. Passolt
	Paul Schatzel
design firm	Visualizer Design Studios
client	The MACgician
	Logo for a Macintosh networking
	solution service.

491

492

493

494

495

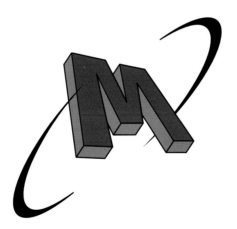

496

497

498

499

500

497
designer   Sarah Tannas
design firm   Tannas Design
client   Cafe Romantico
Proposed logo for a small
Italian cafe.

498
designer   Daren L. Passolt
design firm   Visualizer Design Studios
client   Advantage
Logo created for an online laptop
that provides on-demand
information to the sales force and
field members.

499
designer   Daren L. Passolt
design firm   Visualizer Design Studios
client   Amdahl Corporation
Proposed revision to update the
look of their existing logo.

500
designer   Sarah Tannas
design firm   Tannas Design
client   Amazonia
Logo for an upscale Brazilian
clothing company.

501
designer   Daren L. Passolt
design firm   Visualizer Design Studios
client   Disaster Contingency Solutions
Logo created for a group that
helps companies get up and
running again after any type of
natural disaster.

502
designer   Daren L. Passolt
design firm   Visualizer Design Studios
client   Amdahl Corporation
Created for purchasing department
suppliers guide booklet.

501

502

503

designer	John Smeaton
art director	Scott A. Mednick
design firm	Think New Ideas
client	Upper Deck Authenticated

Logo for a company specializing in authentic sport collectibles.

504

designer	John Smeaton
design firm	Smeaton Design
client	MSA

Logo for architect Mark Smeaton.

505

designer	Daren L. Passolt
design firm	Visualizer Design Studios
client	Repro Graphics

Created for an internal reproduction graphics department.

506

designer	Cheryl Pelly
design firm	Pelly Design Associates for Terry Ruscin Advertising, Inc.
client	Rancho Bernardo Health Center

Logo for a retirement/health care facility.

507

designer	Cheryl Pelly
design firm	C.W.A., Inc.
client	Humetrix

Logo for a manufacturer of instruments that measure human heart rates, blood pressure, etc.

503

504

505

RANCHO BERNARDO
HEALTH CENTER

506

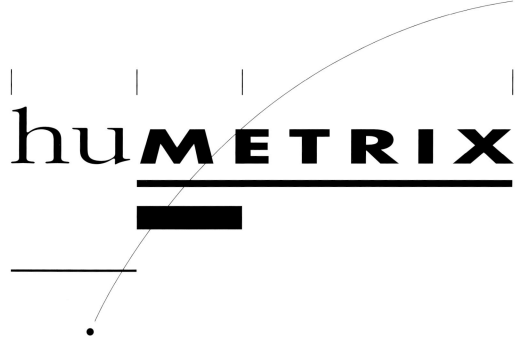

507

508
designers   Mary Evelyn McGough
              Mike Hand
art director Mike Salisbury
design firm Mike Salisbury
              Communications, Inc.
client   Fiction Now

509
designer   Mary Evelyn McGough
art director Mike Salisbury
design firm Mike Salisbury
              Communications, Inc.
client   Mike Salisbury
              Communications, Inc.
              Logo for a graphic design and
              advertising firm.

510
designer   Barbara Bettis
design firm Hamagami/Carroll & Associates
client   DirecTV
              Logo for satellite TV programming
              distributors.

511
designer   Dickson Keyser
design firm Northern California Chapter of
              SEGD
client   Noe Valley Ministry
              Logo for a multi-use community
              center for a San Francisco
              neighborhood.

512
designer   Joe Miller
design firm Joe Miller's Company
client   Works
              Logo for a non-profit alternative art
              and performance space.

513
designer   Lewis Harrison
design firm Lewis Harrison Design, Inc.
client   Cool Cottons
              Logo for a children's casual
              clothing line made only with 100%
              cotton in mostly pastel colors.

508

509

510

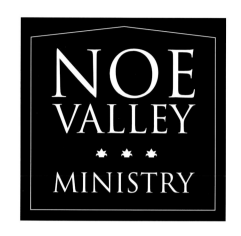

511

512

513

514
designer   Jeff Ishikawa
design firm   GDA Technology Advertising
client   GDA Technology Advertising
               Logo for advertising agency
               specializing in high-tech clients.

515
designer   Leslie Oki
art director   Paul Marciano
design firm   Guess? Inc.
client   Guess? Interactive
               Logo for an apparel company.

516
designer   Dickson Keyser
art director   Nancy Daniels
design firm   The GNU Group
client   Lalka
               Logo for a Sheraton
               hotel/restaurant in
               Warsaw, Poland.

517
designer   Archie Ong
art director   Sam Smidt
design firm   Inhaus Design
client   Neon
               Logo for a non-profit organization's
               online service.

518
designer   Larimie Garcia
design firm   gig
client   Larry A. Garcia Landscape
               Company
               Logo for a landscape installation
               and maintanence company.

519
designer   Edoardo Chavarin
art director   Larimie Garcia
design firm   gig
client   Innovation Snowboards
               Logo for a snowboard
               manufacturer.

520
designer   Jon Lagda
art director   Ron Scheibel
design firm   Hunt, Rook & Scheibel
client   WildStuffs
               Logo for a line of toasted
               ravioli appetizers.

514

515

516

517

LARRY A. GARCIA
LANDSCAPE COMPANY

518

519

520

521
designer   Jon Lagda
design firm   K3/Kato Kreative Koncepts
client   Boomslang
Logo for an alternative rock band.

522
designer   Brian Lorenz
design firm   Lorenz Advertising & Design, Inc.
client   New England Velodrome
Committee
Logo for a fund-raising
committee whose purpose is to
generate interest in the fabrication
of a Boston Velodrome.

523
designer   Tosh Kodama
art director   Justin Carroll
design firm   Hamagami/Carroll & Associates
client   20th Century Fox
Logo for the "Millennium"
television series on the cyclical
nature of life.

524
designer   Margo Chase
art director   Samantha Hart
design firm   Margo Chase Design
client   Gramercy Pictures
Logo for a feature film.

525
designer   Archie Ong
design firm   Inhaus Design
client   Agenda
Logo for a bar/restaurant/
lounge.

526
designer   Veronica See
art director   Ken Anderson
design firm   Fattal & Collins
client   Disney Interactive
Logo for Disney software, a
division of Disney Inc.

521

522

523

four
Weddings
and a funeral

524

525

526

527
designer   Dianne O'Quinn Burke
design firm   Burkarts
client   Logo for the San Luis Obispo
              Art Center.

528
designer   Larimie Garcia
art director Jeri Heiden
design firm   gig
client   A&M Records
              Logo for recording artists.

529
designer   Larimie Garcia
art director Greg Gilmer
design firm   gig
client   Warner Bros. Records
              Logo for a recording artist.

530
designer   Douglas Bogner
art directors   David Kessler
                Jon Ianziti
design firm   Bullzye Design & Marketing
client   The Print Shop Deluxe Sampler
                Graphics
                Logo for an edutainment company
                specializing in CD ROM games and
                educational products.

531
designer   Douglas Bogner
art directors   David Kessler
                Jon Ianziti
design firm   Bullzye Design & Marketing
client   Broderbund
                Logo for an edutainment company
                specializing in CD ROM games and
                educational products.

527

528

529

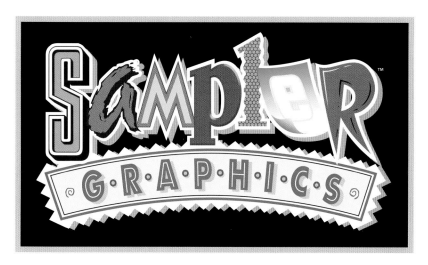

530

531

532
designer	Minka Willig
design firm	Minka Willig Design
client	School of Visual and Performing Arts

Logo for a photography, dance, drama and graphic design school.

533
designer	Mark Orton
art director	John Hamagami
design firm	Hamagami/Carroll & Associates
client	Have A Ball

Logo for a calendar of all scheduled NBA games.

534
designer	Veronica See
art director	Linda Posivak
design firm	Fattal & Collins
client	Castle Rock Entertainment

Logo for motion picture "Othello."

535
designer	Jeni Olsen
art director	Nancy Daniels
design firm	The GNU Group
client	Muju Resort

Logo for a year-round ski and leisure resort in Korea.

536
designer	J. Robert Faulkner
design firm	J. Robert Faulkner Advertising
client	UrbanXtreme

Logo for a line of specialized backpacks.

532

533

534

535

536

537
designer   Veronica See
design firm   Fattal & Collins
client   Play-A Productions
Logo for an educational film/video
production company.

538
designer   Jeff Ivarson
illustrator   Chris Gall
design firm   Ivarson Design Group
client   Andersen Windows
Logo for window
replacement system.

539
designer   Brian Lorenz
design firm   Lorenz Advertising & Design, Inc.
client   Spectranet International
Logo for fiber optics company.

540
designer   Barbara B. Breashears
design firm   B 3 Design
client   Dolce Mia
Logo for handmade frames
and collectibles.

541
designer   Larimie Garcia
design firm   gig
client   Vixen
Logo for a concert poster.

537

538

539

540

541

542
designer   Archie Ong
design firm   Inhaus Design
client   Act Three
          Logo for a contemporary jazz club
          and lounge.

543
designer   Cheri Brewster
art director   Lois Brightwater
design firm   Brightwater Design Inc.
client   Specialty Brands Inc.
          Logo for a new product launch for
          Pacific Tortilla Kitchen.

544
designer   Sarah Tannas
art director   Ron Scheibel
design firm   Hunt, Rook & Scheibel
client   Santa Fe Cafe
          Proposed logo for a line of
          Southwestern entrees.

545
designer   Larimie Garcia
art director   Janet Levinson
design firm   gig
client   Warner Bros. Records
          Logo for "The Black Crowes"
          album cover, entitled "Three
          Snakes and a Charm."

542

543

544

545

Design Studios

A

Addis Group, 93, 335
Aerial, 427, 432, 433, 434, 435, 436, 437, 438, 439, 443
Allen, Mark Design, 143, 278, 379, 399, 401, 409, 410, 411, 412, 415, 420, 428
Armstrong Associates, 265
Atkins, Alexander Design, Inc., 25, 60, 140, 153, 252

B

B 3 Design, 540
B-Square, 85
B.D. Cummings/Illustration, 246, 385
Beller Design, 87
Bielenberg Design Group, 74, 235, 372, 398
Bright Strategic Design, 4, 11, 67, 79, 91, 94, 99, 162, 163, 196, 229, 270, 279, 304, 320, 321, 370, 376, 377, 466
Brightwater Design Inc., 543
Brown, Barbara Marketing and Design, 92, 208, 315
Bullzye Design & Marketing, 75, 76, 530, 531
Burkarts, 527
Burne Design, 388
Buz Design Group, 119, 151, 159, 185, 186, 371, 480, 483

C

C.W.A., Inc., 507
Chase, Margo Design, 41, 194, 239, 342, 524
Coe, Laura Design Associates, 36, 73, 166, 195, 227
Colini, Jeanine Design Associates, 160, 205, 206
Cotsifas/Keyser Design Services, 248, 294, 312

D

DAA, 188
Design Services of Dickson A. Keyser, 241, 286, 387, 419
Designwise, 90, 456
Designworks/USA, 35, 490
Digital Typography & Design, 22
Dowell Design, 442
Dyer/Mutchnick Group Inc., 1, 18, 34, 43, 47, 66, 107, 109, 116, 118, 123, 152, 240, 255, 257, 258, 302, 326, 331, 350, 354, 355, 356, 357, 359, 362, 452, 453, 471, 473, 477, 478

E   F

Edcal Design, 298
Fattal & Collins, 526, 534, 537
Faulkner, J. Robert Advertising, 536
Furman, Martha Newton Design & Illustration, 39, 142, 193, 299, 299A, 351

G

GDA Technology Advertising, 514
Gee + Chung Design, 19, 26
gig, 27, 28, 44, 135, 518, 519, 528, 529, 541, 545
GNU Group, The, 102, 103, 104, 197, 198, 199, 200, 201, 232, 516, 535

Grafico, Miriello, Inc., 5, 218, 330, 484
Gravelle, Carol Graphic Design, 175
Grose, Bradley Design, 171, 179, 180, 181, 182, 183, 184, 242
Guess? Inc., 515
Gunion, Jefrey Illustration & Design, 136, 148

H

Halleck Design Group, 300
Hamagami/Carroll & Associates, 336, 338, 346, 510, 523, 533
Harrison, Lewis Design, Inc., 264, 307, 513
Hausman Design, 20, 21, 23, 45, 287, 303
Hetz Advertising & Design, 189, 220, 253, 259
Hop Art, 446
Hunt, Rook & Scheibel, 82, 155, 202, 203, 204, 345, 520, 544

I   J

Inhaus Design, 9, 517, 525, 542
Ivarson Design Group, 147, 226, 323, 324, 538
JO Design, 469, 470
Juddesign, 8, 169, 344, 348

K

K3 Kato Kreative Koncepts, 112, 521
Kahn Artist Design, 54
Kahn Design, 17, 58, 113, 274, 318
Kelston International, Inc., 125, 126
Komachi, Rick, 178, 275, 451
Kuntz, Diane Design, 69, 84, 95, 96, 97, 217, 316

L   M

Leong, Russell Design, 80, 81, 224, 263, 271, 293, 295, 347, 352, 476
Lewis, Kenneth Design, 343
Lorenz Advertising & Design, Inc., 138, 256, 266, 522, 539
M-Studios, 55, 154, 225, 382, 390, 426
Marshall, Ray Design, 277
Martinez, Glenn and Associates, 2, 10, 29, 37, 63, 211, 212, 231, 251
Mastandrea Design, 214, 308, 349
Matson, Shugart Marketing Communications, 418
McElroy, Darlene Design, 161, 273, 373, 374, 482
Miller's, Joe Company, 301, 327, 333, 512
Mires Design, 24, 56, 111, 129, 133, 167, 170, 172, 173, 216, 234, 237, 238, 261, 262, 267, 284, 285, 291, 292, 305, 309, 332, 417, 421, 422, 423, 424, 425, 429, 430, 431, 441
Mizuno & Associates, 207, 215
Morla Design, 363
Morris, Steven Design, 121, 236, 306, 440
Mortensen Design, 386

Designers

Art Directors and Illustrators

Clients

Special Thanks

I would like to thank Lisa Woodard and Suzanne Rosentswieg for all the help and encouragement they gave me to keep Gerry's series going.

I would like to applaud Arpi Ermoyan for always being patient and understanding and for always getting the job done.

My hat is off to Harish Patel for doing a first class job of organizing and designing this book.